Microsoft® Publisher 2002

Illustrated Essentials

Marjorie Hunt

COURSE
TECHNOLOGY

THOMSON LEARNING™

Australia • Canada • Mexico • Singapore • Spain • United Kingdom • United States

COURSE
TECHNOLOGY
™
THOMSON LEARNING

Microsoft® Publisher 2002 - Illustrated Essentials
Marjorie Hunt

Managing Editor:
Nicole Jones Pinard

Product Manager:
Emily Heberlein

Associate Product Manager:
Emeline Elliott

Production Editor:
Anne Valsangiacomo

Developmental Editor:
Rachel Biheller Bunin

Editorial Assistant:
Christina Kling Garrett

QA Manuscript Reviewers:
John Freitas, Ashlee Welz, Alex
White, Harris Bierhoff, Serge
Palladino, Holly Schabowski, Jeff
Schwartz

Text Designer:
Joseph Lee, Black Fish Design

Composition House:
GEX Publishing Services

The Illustrated Series Vision

Teaching and writing about computer applications can be extremely rewarding and challenging. How do we engage students and keep their interest? How do we teach them skills that they can easily apply on the job? As we set out to write this book, our goals were to develop a textbook that:

- ► works for a beginning student
- ► provides varied, flexible and meaningful exercises and projects to reinforce the skills
- ► serves as a reference tool
- ► makes your job as an educator easier, by providing resources above and beyond the textbook to help you teach your course

Our popular, streamlined format is based on advice from instructional designers and customers. This flexible design presents each lesson on a two-page spread, with step-by-step instructions on the left, and screen illustrations on the right. This signature style, coupled with high-caliber content, provides a comprehensive yet manageable introduction to Microsoft Publisher - it is a teaching package for the instructor and a learning experience for the student.

AUTHOR ACKNOWLEDGMENTS

I would like to thank Nicole Pinard for giving me the opportunity to become an author on this book, Emily Heberlein for her masterful ability to keep us all on track, and Rachel Bunin for her thoughtful editing and constant good humor. I would also like to thank my husband Cecil, whose support, love, and late night snacks gave me the strength to make (most of) my deadlines.

Marjorie Hunt

Preface

Welcome to *Microsoft Publisher 2002– Illustrated Essentials*. Each lesson in this book contains elements pictured to the right in the sample two-page spread.

► How is the book organized?
The book is organized into three units on Publisher. In these units, students will learn how to create and format well-designed, real-world publications for print and for the Web.

► What kinds of assignments are included in the book? At what level of difficulty?
The lessons use MediaLoft, a fictional chain of bookstores, as the case study. The assignments on the blue pages at the end of each unit increase in difficulty. Project files and case studies, with many international examples, provide a great variety of interesting and relevant business applications for skills. Assignments include:

- **Concepts Reviews** include multiple choice, matching, and screen identification questions.

- **Skills Reviews** provide additional hands-on, step-by-step reinforcement.

- **Independent Challenges** are case projects requiring critical thinking and application of the unit skills. The Independent Challenges increase in difficulty, with the first one in each unit being the easiest (most step-by-step with detailed instructions). Subsequent Independent Challenges become increasingly open-ended, requiring more independent problem solving.

- **E-Quest Independent Challenges** are case projects with a Web focus. E-Quests require the use of the World Wide Web to conduct research to complete the project.

- **Visual Workshops** show a completed file and require that the file be created without any step-by-step guidance, involving independent problem solving .

Each 2-page spread focuses on a single skill.

Concise text that introduces the basic principles in the lesson and integrates the brief case study, indicated by the paintbrush icon.

Publisher 2002

Formatting Text

Once you enter text in your publication, you can select it and then apply formatting to enhance its appearance. You can format text using the Formatting toolbar, which includes buttons for boldfacing, italicizing, and underlining text, and for changing text alignment and text color. You can easily change the font style and the font size, the physical size of the characters measured in points, using the Font Size list arrow on the Formatting toolbar. Another formatting feature is AutoFit. AutoFit automatically sizes text to fit it in a text box. Karen formats the text to make the flyer more attractive and readable. She uses the AutoFit feature to resize the Company, she changes the font in other text boxes from Times Roman to Franklin Gothic Demi, then she removes bold formatting.

Steps

1. Click in the Highlights text box, press [F9] to zoom in, select the word **Highlights**, click **Format** on the menu bar, click **AutoFit Text**, then click **Best Fit**
   All the text in the Highlights text box is now bigger, as shown in Figure A-11. The font and font size of the selected text are displayed on the Formatting toolbar. The font is Franklin Gothic Demi and the font size is 26.7.

2. Press [F9] then click in the **For Friday's beach party** text box

3. Press [Ctrl][A] to select all the text in the text box, press [F9] to zoom in then click the font list arrow on the Formatting Toolbar
   The names of the fonts in the Font list are formatted in the font they represent, making it easier for you to choose among them.

   Trouble?
   The font may appear at the top of the font list as well as within the alphabetical list.

4. Scroll the list of fonts, then click **Franklin Gothic Demi Cond** on the Font drop-down list, as shown in Figure A-11
   The selected text changes to Franklin Gothic Demi Condensed.

5. Click in the Highlights text box, select the bulleted items, click the **Font list arrow**, click **Franklin Gothic Demi**, click the arrow to the right of the Font Color button **A**, then click **the black square**
   The bullets now appear in black in Franklin Gothic Demi. The Font Color button now shows the color black, indicating that you can click it to apply black formatting to selected text.

   QuickTip
   Press [Ctrl][B] to quickly bold text after you select it.

6. Scroll down to the bottom of the publication, select **your name, x5140**, then click the **Bold button B** on the Formatting toolbar
   The selected text is now not boldface.

7. Select **11 AM to Dusk**, click **B**, select **July 28**, then click **B**
   The flyer is looking good. The fonts are consistent, and bold is now used to highlight just the headings at the bottom of the flyer.

TABLE A-2: **Common Pointer Shapes**

pointer shape	use to	pointer shape	use to
	Resize an object in the direction of the arrows	+	Draw a frame
	Move an object to a new location		Crop an object
	Drag selected text to a new location		Insert overflow text
	Rotate an object		

Hints as well as troubleshooting advice, right where you need it – next to the step itself.

Quickly accessible summaries of key terms, toolbar buttons, or keyboard alternatives connected with the lesson material. Students can refer easily to this information when working on their own projects at a later time.

Every lesson features large, full-color representations of what the screen should look like as students complete the numbered steps.

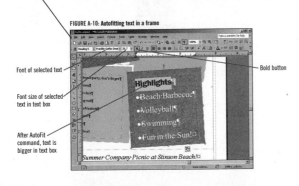

FIGURE A-10: Autofitting text in a frame

Font of selected text

Font size of selected text in text box

After AutoFit command, text is bigger in text box

Bold button

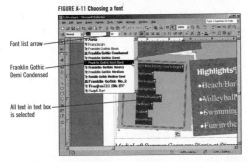

FIGURE A-11 Choosing a font

Font list arrow

Franklin Gothic Demi Condensed

All text in text box is selected

Spell checking your publication

Before you finalize a publication, you should check it for spelling errors. To have Publisher check for spelling errors in your publication, click Tools on the menu bar, point to Spelling, then click Spelling. In the Check Spelling dialog box, shown in Figure A-12, you can choose to ignore or change the words Publisher identifies as misspelled. You can also add a word to the dictionary. To check the spelling in every text box in your publication, make sure the Check all stories check box is selected in the Check Spelling dialog box.

FIGURE A-12: Check Spelling dialog box

Click to check spelling in every text box

Clues to Use boxes provide concise information that either expands on the major lesson skill or describes an independent task that in some way relates to the major lesson skill.

The pages are numbered according to unit. A indicates the unit, 11 indicates the page.

► **What distance learning options are available to accompany this book?**

Visit www.course.com for more information on our Distance Learning materials to accompany Illustrated titles. Options include:

MyCourse.com

Need a quick, simple tool to help you manage your course? Try MyCourse.com, the easiest to use, most flexible syllabus and content management tool available. MyCourse.com offers you brand new content, including Topic Reviews, Extra Case Projects, and Quizzes, to accompany this book.

WebCT

Course Technology and WebCT have partnered to provide you with the highest quality online resources and Web-based tools for your class. Course Technology offers content for this book to help you create your WebCT class, such as a suggested Syllabus, Lecture Notes, Practice Test questions, and more.

Blackboard

Course Technology and Blackboard have also partnered to provide you with the highest quality online resources and Web-based tools for your class. Course Technology offers content for this book to help you create your Blackboard class, such as a suggested Syllabus, Lecture Notes, Practice Test questions, and more.

Instructor Resources

The Instructor's Resource Kit (IRK) CD is Course Technology's way of putting the resources and information needed to teach and learn effectively into your hands. All the components are available on the IRK, (pictured below), and many of the resources can be downloaded from www.course.com.

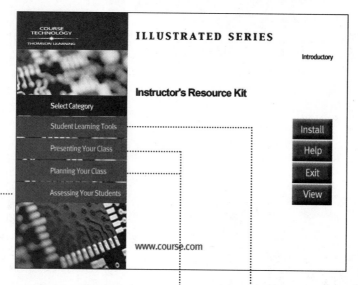

ASSESSING YOUR STUDENTS

Solution Files
Solution Files are Project Files completed with comprehensive sample answers. Use these files to evaluate your students' work. Or, distribute them electronically or in hard copy so students can verify their own work.

ExamView
ExamView is a powerful testing software package that allows you to create and administer printed, computer (LAN-based), and Internet exams. ExamView includes hundreds of questions that correspond to the topics covered in this text, enabling students to generate detailed study guides that include page references for further review. The computer-based and Internet testing components allow students to take exams at their computers, and also save you time by grading each exam automatically.

PRESENTING YOUR CLASS

Figure Files
Figure Files contain all the figures from the book in .jpg format. Use the figure files to create transparency masters or in a PowerPoint presentation.

STUDENT TOOLS

Project Files and Project Files List
To complete most of the units in this book, your students will need **Project Files**. Put them on a file server for students to copy. The Project Files are available on the Instructor's Resource Kit CD-ROM, the Review Pack, and can also be downloaded from www.course.com.

Instruct students to use the **Project Files List** at the end of the book. This list gives instructions on copying and organizing files.

PLANNING YOUR CLASS

Instructor's Manual
Available as an electronic file, the Instructor's Manual is quality-assurance tested and includes unit overviews, detailed lecture topics for each unit with teaching tips, comprehensive sample solutions to all lessons and end-of-unit material, and extra Independent Challenges. The Instructor's Manual is available on the Instructor's Resource Kit CD-ROM, or you can download it from www.course.com.

Sample Syllabus
Prepare and customize your course easily using this sample course outline (available on the Instructor's Resource Kit CD-ROM).

Contents

Publisher

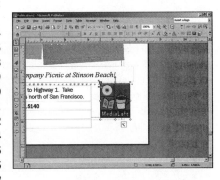

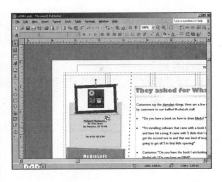

Read This Before You Begin

Software Information and Required Installation

This book was written and tested using Microsoft Publisher 2002, with a typical installation on Microsoft Windows 2000, with Internet Explorer 5.0 or higher. Depending on your installation, the fonts, templates and themes available to you may differ.

Tips for Students

What are Project Files?

You need to use Project Files to complete the lessons and exercises. You use a Project File, which contains a partially completed document used in an exercise, so you don't have to type in all the information you need in the document. Your instructor will either provide you with a copy of the Project Files or ask you to make your own copy. Detailed instructions on how to organize you files, as well as a complete listing of all the files you'll need and will create, can be found in the back of the book (look for the yellow pages) in the Project Files List.

Why is my screen different from the book?

1. Your Desktop components and some dialog box options might be different if you are using an operating system other than Windows 2000

2. Depending on your computer hardware capabilities and the Windows Display settings on your computer, you may notice the following differences:
- Your screen may look larger or smaller because of your screen resolution (the height and width of your screen)
- The colors of the title bar in your screen may be a solid blue

3. Depending on your Office settings, your toolbars may display on a single row and your menus may display with a shortened list of frequently used commands. Office menus and toolbars can modify themselves to your working style by displaying only the most frequently used buttons and menu commands.

Toolbars on one row

To view buttons not currently displayed, click a Toolbar Options button 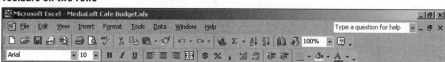 at the end of either the Standard or Formatting toolbar. To view the full list of menu commands, click the double arrow at the bottom of the menu.

In order to have your toolbars display on two rows, showing all buttons, and to have the full menus display, you must turn off the personalized menus and toolbars feature. Click Tools on the menu bar, Click Customize, select the Show Standard and Formatting toolbars on two rows and Always show full menus check boxes on the Options tab, then click Close. This book assumes you are displaying toolbars on two rows and full menus.

Toolbars on two rows

Getting
Started with Publisher 2002

Objectives

► **Define desktop publishing software**
► **Start Publisher and view the Publisher window**
► **Create a publication using an existing design**
► **Replace text in text boxes**
► **Format text**
► **Resize and move objects**
► **Insert a picture**
► **Save, preview, and print a publication**
► **Close a publication and exit Publisher**

Microsoft Publisher 2002 is a desktop publishing program that helps you transform your ideas into visually appealing publications and Web sites for your business, organization, or home. In this unit, you will learn how to use one of Publisher's existing designs to create a publication that includes text and graphics. Then, you will save and print your publication before closing it and exiting Publisher. ⟍ Karen Rosen is the director of human resources at MediaLoft, a nationwide chain of bookstore cafés that sells books, CDs, and videos. Karen is planning the MediaLoft company picnic for the San Francisco–based employees. She uses Publisher to create a flyer announcing the event.

Publisher 2002

Defining Desktop Publishing Software

A **desktop publishing program** lets you integrate text, pictures, drawings, tables, and charts in one document using your personal computer. A document created in Publisher is called a **publication**. You can design a publication from scratch, or you can start with one of Publisher's existing designs and customize it to your needs. Figure A-1 shows three publications created using Publisher's premade designs.  Karen wants the flyer announcing the MediaLoft company picnic to be informative and eye-catching. She decides to create it using one of Publisher's designs. Figure A-2 shows the original design that Karen annotated to show how she will customize it to create the flyer. Karen reviews Publisher's features.

Details

► **Create professionally designed publications**
Publisher includes more than 1,000 premade designs for creating newsletters, flyers, calendars, and many other types of publications. The premade designs include sample text and graphics, a sample layout, and sample color palettes that look great together. You can create publications quickly and easily by starting with a premade design and replacing the text and graphics to suit your needs and tastes. Karen plans on using the Company Picnic flyer design to create the MediaLoft Company picnic flyer.

► **Create a set of publications with a common design**
Publisher includes more than 40 **design sets**, groups of sample publications with the same design theme. You could use a design set to ensure a consistent look for all the printed materials for your company.

► **Change your publication's color scheme**
Publisher includes more than 50 preset color schemes that you can apply to the publications you create using one of Publisher's existing designs. Each color scheme contains five colors that work well together. Karen plans on using the Parrot color scheme in the flyer.

► **Insert text and graphics created in other applications and insert clip art**
You can insert files created in other programs into your publications. You can insert text from a Word file into a company newsletter. You can insert photos, scanned images, or images drawn using Publisher or another drawing program. The Media Gallery, included with Publisher and all Microsoft Office applications, contains thousands of pictures, sounds, and motion clips that you can also add to your publications.

► **Arrange text and graphics easily**
All elements of a publication are **objects**—boxes that contain text or frames that contain graphics that you can easily move, flip, resize, overlap, or color to control the overall appearance of a publication.

► **Choose from preset font schemes and format text easily**
Fonts play a very important role in setting the mood and conveying the message of a publication. A **font** is the typeface or design of a set of characters, such as letters and numbers. Publisher includes 25 **font schemes**, or sets of fonts that look good together. You can also use Publisher's text-formatting features to enhance fonts by adding characteristics such as bold and italics. Karen chooses the Economy font scheme, because it has a casual and fun look.

► **Print publications on your own printer or prepare a publication for commercial printing**
Publisher's commercial printing technology supports process color, spot color and black and white printing, the four major color models (RGB, HSL, CMYK, and PANTONE), and automatic and manual color trapping.

► **Publish to the Web**
You can create professional-looking Web sites using one of Publisher's Web site premade designs. Publisher includes hundreds of Web page backgrounds and animated GIF files. You can also convert an existing publication to a Web page.

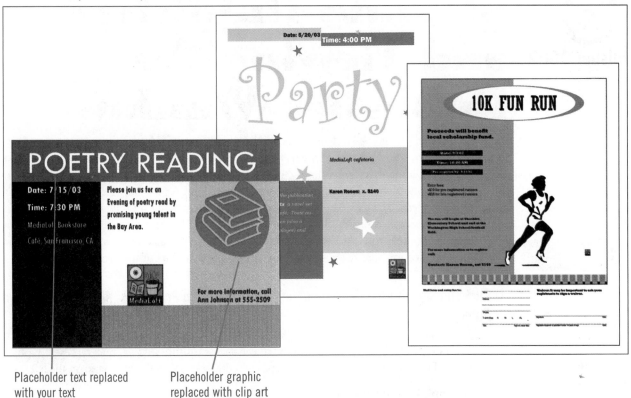

Placeholder text replaced
with your text

Placeholder graphic
replaced with clip art

FIGURE A-2: Karen's notes for modifying the flyer

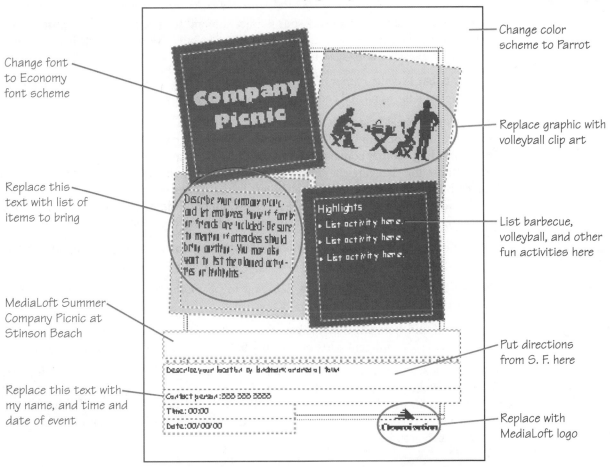

Change font
to Economy
font scheme

Replace this
text with list of
items to bring

MediaLoft Summer
Company Picnic at
Stinson Beach

Replace this text with
my name, and time and
date of event

Change color
scheme to Parrot

Replace graphic with
volleyball clip art

List barbecue,
volleyball, and other
fun activities here

Put directions
from S. F. here

Replace with
MediaLoft logo

Starting Publisher and Viewing the Publisher Window

You start Publisher just as you start any other Windows application—by using the Start menu. When you start Publisher, you see that the screen is divided into two panes. The left pane is called the **task pane**, which is a window that provides the most commonly used commands. Using the task pane, you can create a publication either from scratch or by choosing a premade design and customizing it to meet your needs. The task pane displays different options based on the task you are performing. The right pane, called the **Publications Gallery**, displays thumbnails of existing designs from which you can choose if you don't want to start from scratch.   ▟▀▀▀   Karen starts Publisher, starts a new blank publication, and takes a look at the important elements of the program.

1. Click the **Start button** 🏁 Start on the taskbar, point to **Programs**, then click **Microsoft Publisher**

    Publisher opens. You can see that the screen is divided into two panes, as shown in Figure A-3. The Publication Gallery, on the right side of the screen shows **thumbnails** or small representations, of the Quick Publications, the Publication Type currently selected in the task pane on the left.

2. Click **Blank Publication** in the New section of the task pane

    The task pane and the Publications Gallery close, and a blank one-page publication appears in the publication window, as shown in Figure A-4. The Publisher window displays the following elements:

▶ The **title bar** contains the name of your publication and the program name. Until you save a publication and give it a name, the temporary name is Publication1. The title bar also contains the Minimize, Restore, and Close buttons.

▶ The **menu bar** lists the names of menus that contain Publisher commands. Clicking a menu name displays a list of related commands from which you can choose.

▶ Four **toolbars** appear by default when you start Publisher. The **Standard toolbar** includes buttons for the most commonly used commands, such as opening, saving, or printing a publication. The **Formatting toolbar** contains buttons for the most frequently used formatting commands, such as those for changing the font, and formatting and aligning text. The **Objects toolbar** includes buttons for selecting and creating text boxes, shapes, and picture frames, as well as buttons for working with other types of objects. The **Connect Frames toolbar** gives you options for connecting overflow text from one part of your publication to another.

▶ The **publication window** includes the **publication page** or pages and a **desktop workspace** for storing text and graphics prior to placing them in your publication.

▶ The **vertical and horizontal rulers** help you to position, size, and align text and graphics precisely in your publications.

▶ The **vertical and horizontal scroll bars** work like scroll bars in any Windows program—you use them to display different parts of your publication in the publication window.

▶ The **status bar**, located below the publication window, displays the position and size of the selected object in a publication and shows the current page. You can use the **Page Navigation buttons** to jump to a specific page in your publication. You can use the **Object Position indicator** to precisely position an object containing text or graphics, and the **Object Size indicator** to accurately gauge the size of an object.

FIGURE A-3: Publisher opening screen with task pane open

New Publication task pane

Click to hide Publication Gallery

Click to open a blank presentation

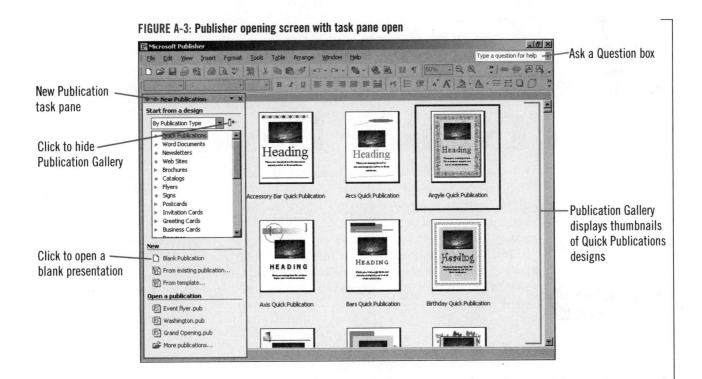

Ask a Question box

Publication Gallery displays thumbnails of Quick Publications designs

FIGURE A-4: Blank one-page publication

Title bar

Standard toolbar

Objects toolbar

Publication window

Vertical ruler

Status bar

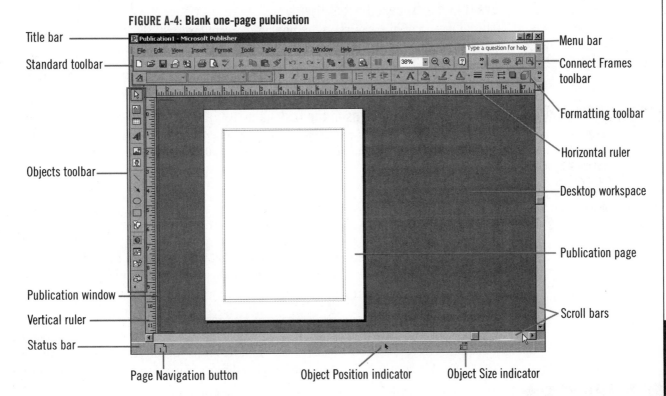

Menu bar

Connect Frames toolbar

Formatting toolbar

Horizontal ruler

Desktop workspace

Publication page

Scroll bars

Page Navigation button

Object Position indicator

Object Size indicator

TABLE A-1: Task pane options available when starting a new publication

area of task pane	options available
Start from a design	Click a publication type from the list, then click a design in the Publication Gallery
New	Start a blank publication from scratch, from an existing publication, or from a template
Open a publication	Open a publication that has been recently opened by clicking its name on the list or click More publications to find a publication on your computer

Publisher 2002

Creating a Publication Using an Existing Design

Although you can always start from scratch, the easiest way to create a publication is to start from an existing design and then modify it to meet your needs and preferences. Publisher provides hundreds of premade designs all containing sample layouts, font schemes, graphics, and colors schemes. You can use the New by Design or the New by Publication Type options in the task pane to access these designs. Some of the objects in a premade design contain **wizards**, which ask you questions about the information you want to include in your publication, and then customize the object according to your answers. You start a new publication by using the New Publication task pane. ✎ Karen decides to create the flyer for the company picnic by starting with an existing design.

1. Click **File** on the menu bar, then click **New**
   The task pane opens, displaying options for creating a new publication.

Trouble?

If you don't see any thumbnails click the Show Publication Gallery button 🖅 next to the By Publication Type list arrow.

2. Click **Flyers** in the By Publication Type list at the top of the task pane, then click **Event** in the expanded list of flyer types
   The Publication Gallery displays thumbnails of Event Flyers, as shown in Figure A-5.

3. Click the **Company Picnic Flyer** in the Publications Gallery
   The Company Picnic flyer appears in the publication window. The task pane now displays options for modifying the layout of the flyer.

Trouble?

If a Publisher dialog box opens asking you to enter information about yourself, click OK, then click Cancel in the Personal Information dialog box that appears.

4. Click **Publication Designs** in the task pane
   The Publications Designs task pane displays flyers with the Company Picnic flyer design selected. You can apply a new design at this point by clicking to any one of the designs listed.

5. Click **Color Schemes** in the task pane
   The Apply a color scheme list appears in the task pane. Each color scheme includes five colors that work well together. Trout is the color scheme selected by default for the Company Picnic flyer design.

6. Scroll through the alphabetical list of color schemes, then click **Parrot**
   The Parrot color scheme is applied to the flyer in the publication window.

7. Click **Font Schemes** in the task pane
   A list of named font schemes appears in the task pane, showing 25 predefined sets of fonts that work well together. Font schemes make it possible to change the look of your publication quickly, assigning all text that are major fonts to one style, and all text that are in a minor font to another, ensuring that fonts will be applied consistently throughout your publication.

QuickTip

If you don't like the choice of color scheme or font scheme, you can click the Undo button on the toolbar, then click Undo Color Scheme or Undo Font Scheme.

8. Scroll down the list of font schemes, then click **Economy**
   The new font scheme that includes the Franklin Gothic Demi font and Times New Roman bold is applied to the company picnic flyer. Compare your screen to Figure A-6.

9. Click the task pane **Close button**
   The task pane closes, and the publication window expands to give you more room to work.

FIGURE A-5: Event flyers displayed in Publication Gallery

New Publication task pane

Types of publications listed here

Click to open blank presentation

Click to open a saved publication

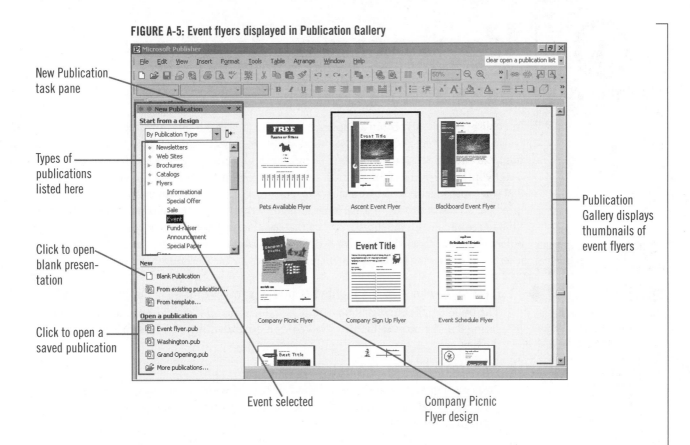

Publication Gallery displays thumbnails of event flyers

Event selected

Company Picnic Flyer design

FIGURE A-6: Company Picnic flyer with Parrot Color scheme and Economy font scheme

Font Schemes task pane

Click to choose a color scheme

Click to choose Economy font scheme

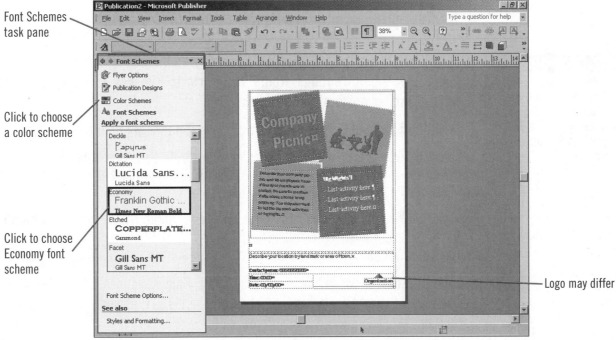

Logo may differ

Publisher 2002

Publisher 2002

Replacing Text in Text Boxes

In Publisher, every element in a publication is contained in a frame. A **frame** is an object that contains text or graphics. A **text box** is a frame that holds text. Before you type in a Publisher publication, you must first create a text box to hold text. Once you create a text box, you can type text directly into it, or you can insert text from a Word document file into it. To enter text in a text box, first you must select it. When you click a text box to select it, **handles** (small circles) appear around its edges. To insert text from a Word document right-click the text box, then use the Change text from file command on the shortcut menu that appears. ✎ Karen is ready to replace the placeholder text in the flyer with her own text. She types some of the text directly into the text boxes and inserts text describing the company picnic from a Word file she created last week.

Steps 1 2 3 4

1. Click in the center of the **Highlights text box** to select the List Activity placeholder text
   The bulleted placeholder items are selected and handles appear around the text box, indicating that the box itself is also selected. You use the white round handles to resize and move the text box.

2. Press **[F9]**
   Pressing [F9] zooms in on the selected section of your publication, making it easier to see your work in detail. The [F9] key is a **toggle key**—press it once to zoom in, then press it again to zoom back out.

3. Type **Beach Barbecue**, press **[Enter]**, type **Volleyball**, press **[Enter]**, type **Swimming**, press **[Enter]**, then type **Fun in the Sun!**

4. Select the text in the **rectangular text box** below the Highlights text box, then type **MediaLoft Summer Company Picnic at Stinson Beach!**
   The text you typed replaces the placeholder text and takes on the default formatting for the text box.

5. Click in the **Describe your location text box** to select the placeholder text in the frame, then type **Directions: Route 101 North to Highway 1. Take Stinson Beach exit—23 miles north of San Francisco**

6. Select **555 555 5555**, type **your name**, press **[Spacebar]** then type **x5140**

7. Select **00:00**, type **11 AM to dusk**, select **00/00/00**, then type **July 28**
   If you are writing long stories, it's sometimes easier to create the document in Word then insert the file into a text frame in Publisher.

8. Right-click in the blue **Describe your company picnic frame**, point to **Change Text** on the shortcut menu, then click **Text File**
   The Insert Text dialog box opens. You need to locate and then select the file you plan to insert.

9. Click the **Look in list arrow** in the Insert Text dialog box, locate the drive and folder where your Project Files are stored, click the file **PB A-1**, as shown in Figure A-7, then click **OK**
   The placeholder text is replaced with the text from the Word file. Notice that the font of the imported text is in the Economy font scheme.

10. Press **[F9]** to zoom out, if necessary
    Compare your flyer with Figure A-8.

FIGURE A-7: Insert Text dialog box

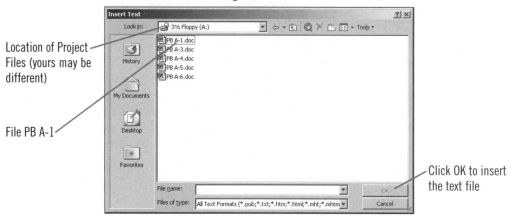

Location of Project Files (yours may be different)

File PB A-1

Click OK to insert the text file

FIGURE A-8: Company Picnic flyer with placeholder text replaced

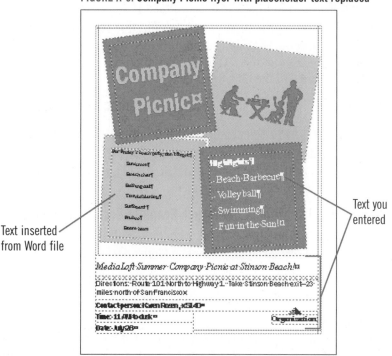

Text inserted from Word file

Text you entered

Creating text boxes

If you need additional text boxes in your publication, or if you are creating a publication from scratch, you can create a new text box easily. To create a text box, click the Text Box button 🔲 on the Objects toolbar. The pointer changes to a crosshair pointer +. Position the pointer where you want one corner of the text frame to appear, press and hold the mouse button, then drag diagonally to create a rectangular frame, as shown in Figure A-9. Release the mouse button when the text box is the size and shape that you want. Then you can enter text in the text box by clicking in the frame and typing or inserting a Word file.

FIGURE A-9: Creating a text box

Text box tool button

Outline of new text frame

Crosshair pointer

Formatting Text

Once you enter text in your publication, you can select it and then apply formatting to enhance its appearance. You can format text using the Formatting toolbar, which includes buttons for boldfacing, italicizing, and underlining text, and for changing text alignment and text color. You can easily change the font style and the **font size**, the physical size of the characters measured in points, using the Font Size list arrow on the Formatting toolbar. Another formatting feature is AutoFit. **AutoFit** automatically sizes text to fit it in a text box. ✐ Karen formats the text to make the flyer more attractive and readable. She uses the AutoFit feature to resize text, she changes the font in other text boxes from Times Roman to Franklin Gothic Demi, then she removes bold formatting.

Steps 1 2 3 4

1. Click in the Highlights text box, press **[F9]** to zoom in, select the word **Highlights**, click **Format** on the menu bar, click **AutoFit Text**, then click **Best Fit**

   All the text in the Highlights text box is now bigger, as shown in Figure A-10. The font and font size of the selected text are displayed on the Formatting toolbar. The font is Franklin Gothic Demi and the font size is 26.7.

2. Press **[F9]** then click in the **For Friday's beach party text box**

3. Press **[Ctrl][A]** to select all the text in the text box, press **[F9]** to zoom in then click the **Font list arrow** on the Formatting Toolbar

   The names of the fonts in the Font list are formatted in the font they represent, making it easier for you to choose among them.

4. Scroll the list of fonts, then click **Franklin Gothic Demi Cond** on the Font drop-down list, as shown in Figure A-11

   The selected text changes to Franklin Gothic Demi Condensed.

5. Click in the Highlights text box, select the bulleted items, click the **Font list arrow**, click **Franklin Gothic Demi**, click the **Font Color list arrow** then click **the black square**

   The bullets now appear in black in Franklin Gothic Demi. The Font Color button now shows the color black, indicating that you can click it to apply black formatting to selected text.

6. Scroll down to the bottom of the publication, select **your name, x5140**, then click the **Bold button** 🅱 on the Formatting toolbar

   The selected text is now not boldface.

7. Select **11 AM to Dusk**, click 🅱, select **July 28**, then click 🅱

   The flyer is looking good. The fonts are consistent, and bold is now used to highlight just the headings at the bottom of the flyer.

FIGURE A-10: Autofitting text in a frame

Font of selected text

Font size of selected text in text box

After AutoFit command, text is bigger in text box

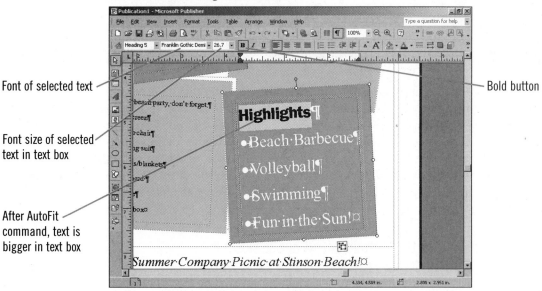

Bold button

FIGURE A-11: Choosing a font

Font list arrow

Franklin Gothic Demi Condensed

All text in text box is selected

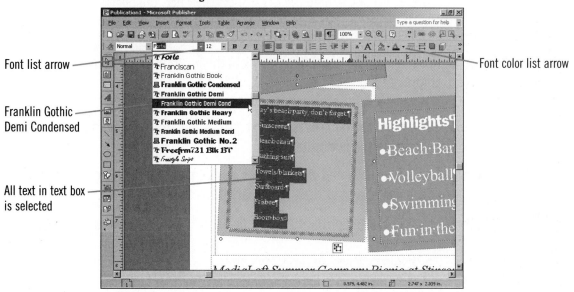

Font color list arrow

Spell checking your publication

Before you finalize a publication, you should check it for spelling errors. To have Publisher check for spelling errors in your publication, click Tools on the menu bar, point to Spelling, then click Spelling. In the Check Spelling dialog box, shown in Figure A-12, you can choose to ignore or change the words Publisher identifies as misspelled. You can also add a word to the dictionary. To check the spelling in every text box in your publication, make sure the Check all stories check box is selected in the Check Spelling dialog box.

FIGURE A-12: Check Spelling dialog box

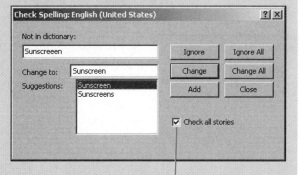

Click to check spelling in every text box

Resizing and Moving Objects

In the course of creating a publication, you might find it necessary to resize or move objects. For example, you might want to make a text box smaller because there is too much white space, or you might want to move a picture closer to its caption. To move or resize an object you must first select it. To resize an object, you drag a handle. To move an object you click anywhere on the object (except on a handle) and drag it to a new location. Karen resizes the text boxes at the bottom of the flyer to align their right edges. She also decides to move the picture frame up and to the right so that it doesn't overlap the blue text box.

Steps

1. **Click the Directions text box to select it**
   Handles appear around the edges of the text box.

2. **Position the pointer over the middle-right handle**
   When you position the pointer over a handle, a Resize pointer appears. Depending on the handle, the pointer will be either a horizontal, vertical, or diagonal resize pointer. See Table A-2 for a list of common pointer shapes. The rulers can be used as guides to precisely align objects as you resize and move them. A line will move along the ruler as you move the object, to guide your placement.

Trouble?

If the rulers do not appear, click View on the menu bar, then click Rulers.

3. **Drag the middle-right handle left to the 6" mark on the horizontal ruler, as shown in Figure A-13**
   The text automatically wraps to fill the resized text box area.

4. **Select the Contact person text box, then drag the middle-right handle to the 6" mark on the horizontal ruler**

5. **Resize the Time and Date frames to align their right edge with the 6" mark on the horizontal ruler and the Contact and Directions text boxes**

QuickTip

To change the length and width of a frame at the same time, drag a corner handle. To keep the center of the frame in the same location, press [Ctrl] as you drag.

6. **Scroll to the top of the flyer and position the pointer over the picnic graphic in the blue frame**
   The pointer changes to the Move pointer ⛟. You use this pointer to move any Publisher object.

7. **Click and drag the picnic graphic up and to the right slightly until it doesn't touch the other blue frame, then release the mouse button**
   You actually dragged two objects at once. This is because the frame and the graphic are grouped together, as indicated by the Ungroup objects button 🔲 located just below the blue frame. The handles still surround the blue frame, with a green rotation handle at the top. You can adjust the angle of any object by dragging the rotation handle.

QuickTip

If you make a mistake, click the Undo button 🔙 on the Standard toolbar.

8. **Drag the rotation handle of the picnic frame to the right ¼", then press [F9] to zoom out and see the entire publication**
   The blue picture frame is now more sharply angled. Compare your screen to Figure A-14.

FIGURE A-13: Resizing an object

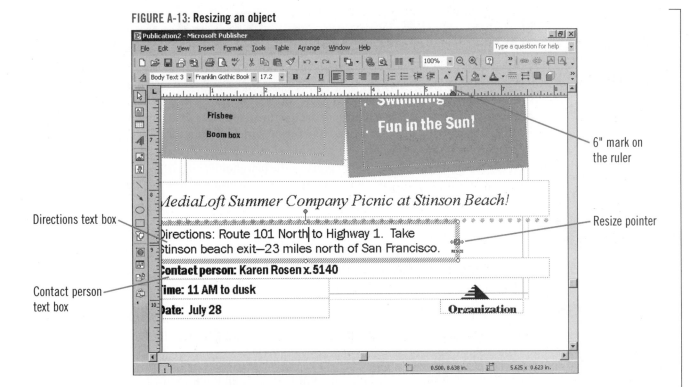

Directions text box

Contact person text box

6" mark on the ruler

Resize pointer

FIGURE A-14: Moving and rotating object

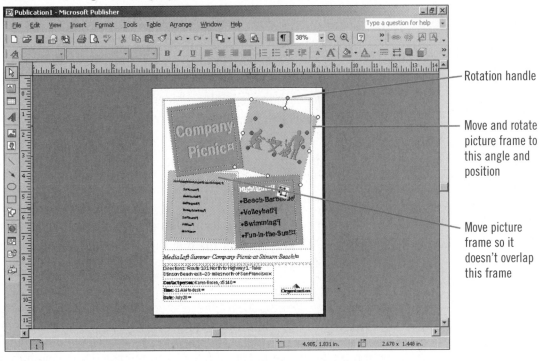

Rotation handle

Move and rotate picture frame to this angle and position

Move picture frame so it doesn't overlap this frame

TABLE A-2: Common Pointer Shapes

pointer shape	use to	pointer shape	use to
	Resize an object in the direction of the arrows	+	Draw a frame
	Move an object to a new location		Crop an object
	Drag selected text to a new location		Insert overflow text
	Rotate an object		

Publisher 2002

Inserting a Picture

Publications usually include both text and graphics. With Publisher, you can insert many types of graphic images into your publications, including clip art, images created in other applications (such as a logo or a chart), scanned images, or photographs taken with a digital camera. The Microsoft **Clip Organizer** is a library of art, pictures, sounds, video clips, and animations that all Office applications share. You can easily preview images from the Clip Organizer and insert them into your publications. Also, you can insert other images that are stored on a disk directly into your publication. ◢▬▬ Karen replaces the placeholder clip art in the flyer with an image of a volleyball in motion from the Clip Organizer. She also replaces the placeholder logo with the MediaLoft logo.

1. Click **View** on the menu bar, then click **Task Pane**
   The task pane opens.

Trouble?

If the Add Clips to gallery dialog box appears asking if you would like to catalog all your media files, click Later.

2. Click the blue frame containing the picnic graphic, click the **picnic graphic** to select it, right-click the **picnic graphic**, point to **Change Picture**, then click **Clip Art**
   The Insert Clip Art task pane opens.

3. Click in the **Search text box**, type **volleyball**, then click **Search**
   The Results window in the task pane appears, and images relating to volleyball appear. It may take a minute or two to display all the images.

Trouble?

If you don't see the image shown in Figure A-15, click another image.

4. Click the first **volleyball image** in the Results window
   The volleyball image replaces the picnic table image on the flyer, as shown in Figure A-15. Your search results may be different.

5. Click the **logo placeholder** in the lower-right corner of the flyer, then click the **Wizard button** ⊠ beneath the logo placeholder
   The Logo Designs task pane opens. You can use these options to create a new logo or to modify an existing one.

6. Click **Logo Options** in the task pane, click **Inserted picture**, then click **Choose picture**
   The Insert Picture dialog box opens.

7. Click the **Look in list arrow**, locate the drive and folder where your Project Files are stored, click **PB A-2**, wait for the preview of the image to appear, then click **Insert**
   The MediaLoft logo replaces the placeholder in the flyer.

8. Close the task pane

9. Press **[F9]** to zoom in on the logo if necessary, drag the **upper-left handle** to resize the logo picture frame until it reaches 6" on the horizontal ruler and 8½" on the vertical ruler, as shown in Figure A-16, then release the mouse button
   Congratulations, you have successfully completed the flyer!

FIGURE A-15: Clip Art search results

Click to insert this image in flyer

Results of search for volleyball images. Your results might be different

Volleyball image replaces picnic image in frame

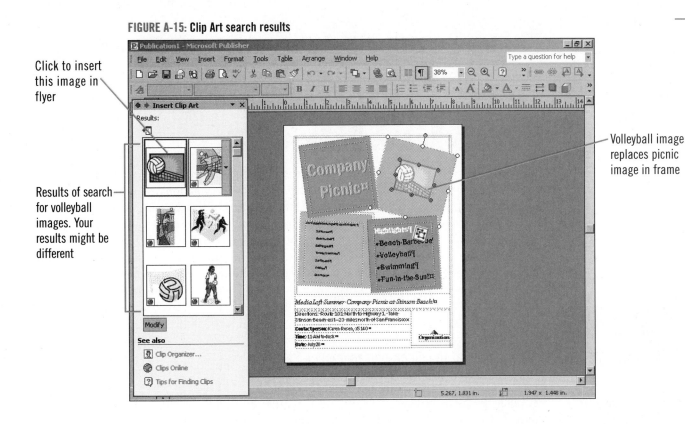

FIGURE A-16: Resizing MediaLoft's logo

Logo sized to 8½" mark on vertical ruler

Resize pointer

Publisher 2002

Saving, Previewing, and Printing a Publication

You need to save your work in order to store it permanently on a disk. You should save your work every 10 to 15 minutes, after any significant changes that you don't want to lose, and before you print your publication. By default, Publisher automatically saves your work every 10 minutes, so you can take advantage of the AutoRecover feature if you lose power or if you have a system problem. To save a file for the first time, you can use the Save or Save As command, or click the Save button on the Standard toolbar. After you've named the file, you must save any new changes to the publication. Once you have saved a publication, you can print it using the Print command. It's a good idea to proofread your publication before you print so that you can catch and fix any mistakes. ✐ Karen saves the flyer, checks it for mistakes, then prints it so she can distribute it to the MediaLoft employees.

QuickTip

After you've saved your publication for the first time, click the Save button 🖫 on the Standard toolbar to quickly save changes to your publication.

1. Click **File** on the menu bar, then click **Save**
   The Save As dialog box opens.

2. Click the **Save in list arrow**, locate the drive and folder where your Project Files are stored, type **Picnic** in the File name text box, compare your dialog box with Figure A-17, then click **Save**

3. Click **No** in the alert box that opens asking if you want to add the MediaLoft logo to your personal information set

4. Click **View** on the menu bar, point to **Zoom**, then click **Whole Page**
   The zoom level adjusts so that the whole page fits in the publication window. When you change the zoom level, you can select a specific zoom percentage, or a specific view. You can also click the Zoom list arrow on the Standard toolbar to change the zoom level.

QuickTip

Press [Ctrl][P] to quickly access the Print dialog box. Click the Print button 🖨 on the Standard toolbar to print the publication with the current settings.

5. Click **File** on the menu bar, then click **Print**
   The Print dialog box opens, as shown in Figure A-18.

6. Make sure the number of copies is **1**, then click **OK**
   Your publication prints in color if you have a color printer, or in black and white if you don't have a color printer. Figure A-19 shows a copy of the completed flyer.

Using the Pack and Go Wizard

When you want to take your publication to another computer or to a commercial printing service, you can use the Pack and Go Wizard to assemble and compress all the files necessary for viewing and printing your publication in a different location. Packing your publication (that is, including the fonts and graphics that you used in your publication) ensures that it will look the same on another computer as it does on yours. If you're packing your publication to disks, Publisher automatically compresses and splits the files so they fit on multiple disks and includes a program to unpack the files on other computers. To use the Pack and Go Wizard, click File on the menu bar, point to Pack and Go, then click Take to Another Computer or Take to a Commercial Printing Service. Read the Wizard screens and make your selections, click Next after each choice, then click Finish when you have answered all of the Wizard's questions.

FIGURE A-17: **Save As dialog box**

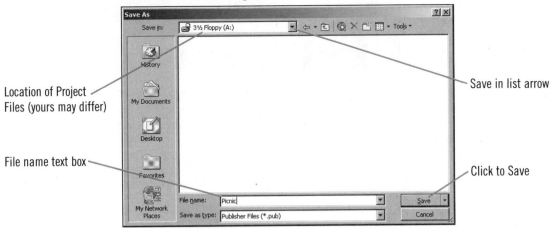

Location of Project
Files (yours may differ)

Save in list arrow

File name text box

Click to Save

FIGURE A-18: **Print dialog box**

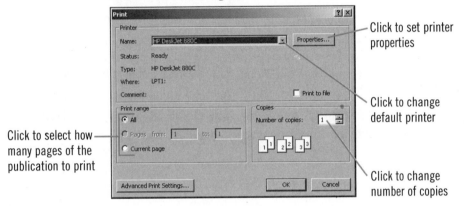

Click to set printer
properties

Click to change
default printer

Click to select how
many pages of the
publication to print

Click to change
number of copies

FIGURE A-19: **Completed publication**

Publisher 2002

Closing a Publication and Exiting Publisher

When you are finished working on a publication, you need to close it. You close a publication by using the Close command on the File menu. When you are finished working with Publisher, you can exit the program by using the Exit command on the File menu. ✐ Karen closes the flyer and exits Publisher.

Steps 1 2 3 4

1. Click **File** on the menu bar, then click **Close**, as shown in Figure A-21

2. If an alert box appears asking if you want to save changes before closing, click **Yes** to save your changes
   The flyer closes and a new, blank publication appears in the Publisher window. You can create a new publication or open an existing publication. If you are finished working with Publisher, you can exit the program.

3. Click **File** on the menu bar, then click **Exit**, as shown in Figure A-22
   The program closes; Publisher is no longer running.

FIGURE A-20: **Office Assistant**

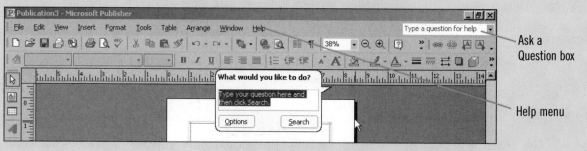

Ask a Question box

Help menu

FIGURE A-21: **Closing a publication**

File menu

Click to close a
publication

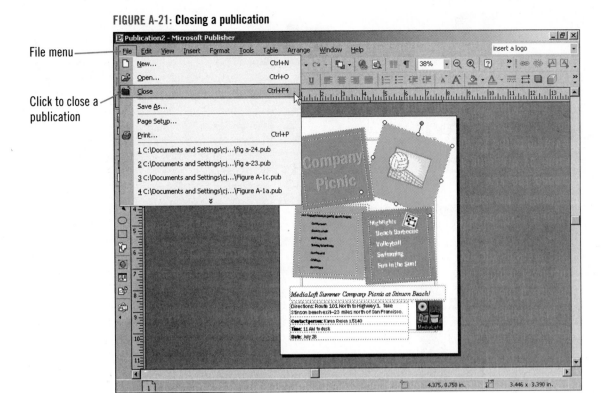

FIGURE A-22: **Exiting Publisher**

Click to close
publication and
exit Publisher at
the same time

Click to exit
Publisher

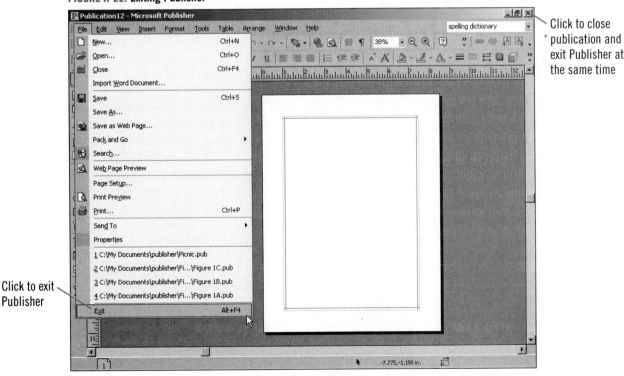

Practice

► Concepts Review

Label each element of the Publisher window shown in Figure A-23.

FIGURE A-23

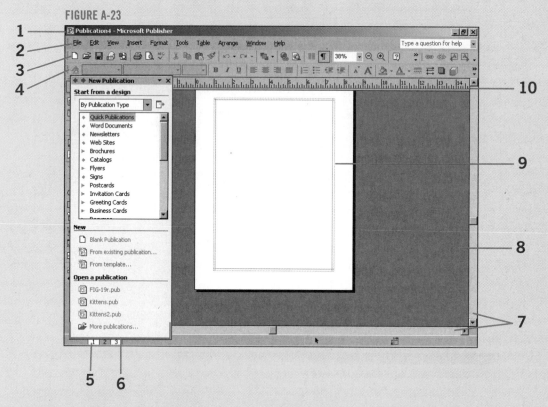

Match each term with the statement that describes it.

11. **Clip Organizer**
12. **Color scheme**
13. **Handles**
14. **Text box**
15. **Font scheme**

a. Object that contains the words in the publication, and can be moved or resized

b. Library of art, pictures, sounds, video, and animations that all Office programs share

c. Preset colors used consistently throughout a publication

d. Preset fonts used consistently throughout a publication

e. Circles that appear around a frame to indicate it is selected

► Skills Review

1. **Start Publisher and view the Publisher window.**
   a. Start Publisher and open a blank publication.
   b. Identify as many parts of the publication window as you can without referring to the unit material.

2. **Create a publication using an existing design.**
   a. Start a new publication.
   b. In the task pane, select the Apartment for Rent Flyer from the Sale Flyers category.

   c. Change the color scheme to Tropics.

   d. Change the font scheme to Facet, which includes the font Gil Sans MT.

3. Replace text in text boxes.

   a. Close the task pane, zoom as needed, then type **6/1/03** for the Available date.

   b. Select the Amount of rent text box, then type the following information, pressing [Enter] after each bullet except the last:

     $1,000/month, 12-month lease, $2,000 deposit required, 2 bedrooms, 2 bathrooms, View of ocean, Access to boat dock, Nonsmokers only, 10-minute walk to shopping.

   c. Select the Describe your location text box, then insert into the text box the text file PB A-3.

   d. Select the text in the Contact person frame, and replace the text with **Call your name for more information: (978) 555-1000**.

   e. Select one of the tear-off Name text boxes at the bottom of the flyer, then type your name and the phone number **(978) 555-1000**. (*Hint*: Click a text box to select it, then start typing.)

   f. Click another tear-off Name text box to update all the other text boxes with your name and phone number.

4. Format text.

   a. Select the first tear-off Your Name text box, then press [Ctrl][A] to select all of the text in the frame.

   b. Bold the text in that text box, then click another Your Name text box to format all the other text boxes.

   c. Italicize the text in the Available frame. (*Hint*: Scroll if necessary to locate the frame.)

   d. Reduce the font size of the text in the $1,000/month text box to 14 points. (*Hint*: Click the Decrease Font Size button on the Formatting toolbar.)

   e. Change the text color of the Call your name text box to red. (*Hint*: Use the Font Color button on the Formatting toolbar to choose another color in the scheme.)

   f. Select the Located in text box, press [Ctrl][A], then format the text to AutoFit, best fit.

5. Resize and move objects.

   a. Drag the right-middle resizing handle of the Located in frame to the 4¼" mark on the horizontal ruler.

   b. Select the Call Your Name text box, drag the middle-left resizing handle to the 4¼" mark on the horizontal ruler.

   c. Drag the Call Your Name text box up to the 7" mark on the vertical ruler to position it next to the Located in text box.

   d. Select the Located in text box and drag the lower-middle resizing handle down to the 8" mark on the vertical ruler. The text automatically resizes because you set it to AutoFit.

   e. Press [F9] to zoom back out and see more of your publication.

6. Insert a picture.

   a. Double-click the house picture frame at the top of the flyer to open the Insert Clip Art task pane. (If a dialog box opens asking if you want to catalog your media files, click Later. If the Format AutoShape dialog box opens, you clicked the graphic. Close the dialog box and try again.)

   b. Type **apartment** in the Search box, click Search, then insert one of the images in the Results box.

   c. Close the Insert Clip Art task pane, then resize the image if necessary.

7. Save, preview, and print a publication.

   a. Save the publication as **Apartment** to the drive and folder where your Project Files are located.

   b. Switch to Whole Page view to proof your publication and make any last-minute changes.

   c. Save your changes, then print your publication.

8. Close a publication and exit Publisher.

   a. Close the publication, then exit Publisher.

▶ Independent Challenge 1

Your cat has just had kittens and you would like to place them in good homes. You decide to use a Publisher template to create a flyer to post at the local veterinary clinic.

a. Start Publisher, use the New from Existing Publication task pane and select the Pets Available Flyer from the Sale Flyers category.

b. Using Figure A-24 as a guide, replace the placeholder text and format that text. Use the Wildflower color scheme.

c. Replace the Describe text frame with the text file PB A-4.

d. Replace the placeholder kitten graphic with a cat of your choosing from the Media Gallery and size the image appropriately.

e. Replace the name Trey with Your Name in the Please call text box and in the tear-off Kittens frames.

f. Save the publication as **Kittens**.

g. Proof the flyer for mistakes, print and close the publication, then exit Publisher.

FIGURE A-24

▶ Independent Challenge 2

You've volunteered to create a home page for your son's elementary school's Web site.

a. Start Publisher, then choose the School Web Site design from the Web Sites category in the New Publication task pane.

b. Choose Sunrise as the color scheme, and Galley as the font scheme.

c. Replace the placeholder text with the text in Table A-3. (*Hint*: Click No in the Autoflow dialog box.)

d. Increase the size of the Vision text box by dragging the lower-middle resizing handle to the 8½" mark on the vertical ruler. Autofit the text.

e. Delete the empty text box at the bottom of the page under the School address frame. Increase the size of the school address frame by dragging the bottom edge of the frame to the 13" mark on the vertical ruler.

f. Apply bold formatting to Vision and Mission, and change the text color to Red. (*Hint*: Use the Font Color button.)

g. Delete the placeholder logo.

h. Save the publication as **Washington**.

i. Proof your publication, print and close the publication, then exit Publisher.

TABLE A-3

placeholder text frame	replace with
Home Page Title	**Washington Elementary School**
Your home page….	Text File PB A-5 (Click No to have Publisher fit the text.)
Your business tag line here	**Making Education Count!** (*Hint*: Resize frame so that text fits.)
Frame below "To contact us"	*Your Name* **Washington Elementary School** **23 School Street** **Waverly, WA 98722**

▶ Independent Challenge 3

Create a calendar for next month using a Publisher template.

a. Start Publisher, click the Calendar category, then select a full-page calendar template from the New Publication task pane.

b. On the Calendar options task pane, choose the monthly option and change the date range from the beginning of next month to the end of next month. Do not include a schedule of events.

c. Choose a color and font scheme of your choice.

d. Replace the placeholder text with text of your own, making sure to include your name somewhere on the calendar. Format the text appropriately, and customize the logo if a logo placeholder is part of the template. Replace any clip art with appropriate images.

e. Save the publication as **Calendar**. Click No if asked to save the logo to the Primary Business personal information set.

f. Proofread and spell check your publication, print and close the publication, then exit Publisher.

Independent Challenge 4

You own a small travel agency and have put together a five-day tour package to London. You plan to create a brochure providing information to prospective tour guests about the package. To complete the flyer, you will first need to do some research on the Internet about London.

a. Use a search engine site such as Google (www.google.com) or AltaVista (www.altavista.com) and research the following information:
1. Name and street address of 5-star hotel
2. Name of art museum, with specific exhibit mentioned
3. Name of another museum that is not art-related
4. Shopping at <insert names of two shopping districts or stores>
5. One nightlife activity (such as a cabaret, disco, or comedy club) providing the name of the locale
6. Sightseeing activity of your choosing.

When you've gathered all your information, you are ready to create the flyer. To create the flyer:

b. Start Publisher. In the New Publication task pane, select the 3 Picture Product Flyer in the Sale Flyers category.

c. Replace the Product Title Placeholder text with **5 Days in London**. Replace the text in the Product Heading text box with **Theatre, museums, and more!**

d. In the text box directly below Theatre, museums, and more! replace the placeholder text with file PB A-6. Click No in the autoflow dialog box, then resize the text box so the text fits. Change the font to Franklin Gothic Book 12 point.

e. In the List feature here frame, replace the placeholder bullets with six bullets of your own, providing information on the items you researched. Use step A as a guide for creating the bullets.

f. Replace the three placeholder graphics on the flyer with clip art images from the Clip Organizer.

g. Include a logo at the bottom of the flyer for Cultural Excursions, Inc., using the Font Focus logo.

h. In the Contact person frame, replace the placeholder text with **Call Your Name for pricing and reservations**. Add a phone number.

i. Save the flyer as **London**.

j. Check the spelling, print and close the publication, then exit Publisher.

▶ Visual Workshop

Create the flyer shown in Figure A-25 using the Ascent Event design in the Event Flyer category. Use the Field color scheme and the Verbatim font scheme. Replace the placeholder photo and graphics with the clip art shown. (*Hint:* Open the Insert Clip Art task pane, then search for **Fish**. If the images shown are not available, choose other ones.) Drag the green rotation handle to rotate the fish in the green and black rectangles 90 degrees to the right. To create the logo, click the Logo Wizard button to open the Logo Designs task pane, then choose the Open Oval design. (*Hint:* To add the fish graphic to the logo at the bottom of the page, right-click the graphic placeholder, click Change Picture, click Clip Art to open the Insert Clip Art task pane, then type **fish** in the Search text box.) Add your name to the Call frame. Autofit the text in every frame except the Date, Time, and Call Your Name frames. Save the publication as **Grand Opening** in the drive and folder where your Project Files are stored, then print a copy.

FIGURE A-25

Working

with Text and Graphics

Objectives

- ► **Plan a publication**
- ► **Create columns of text**
- ► **Work with overflow text**
- ► **Use guides**
- ► **Create picture captions**
- ► **Create headers and footers**
- ► **Insert and format WordArt**
- ► **Wrap text around objects**
- ► **Layer and group objects**

Publisher provides you with a wide array of tools to help you work with text and graphics. In this unit, you will learn how to create a newsletter. You will place text in columns and learn how to manage text that doesn't all fit in one text box. Then, you will insert a caption for a picture and learn how to wrap text around that and other objects. You will learn how to insert headers and footers that appear on every page of your publication. You will also create and format WordArt and learn about layering and grouping objects. Karen Rosen produces a quarterly newsletter called *LoftLife* for MediaLoft employees. Karen starts by planning the content of the newsletter. Then, she uses the skills covered in this unit to create it.

Planning a Publication

Before creating a publication, you must first plan its design and content. Careful planning helps to ensure that your publication will be both informative and eye-catching. ✎➤ Before she starts working on the newsletter, Karen plans the next edition of the *LoftLife* newsletter. Figure B-1 shows Karen's plan for the content, graphics, and layout.

▶ What layout to use

Choosing the layout is the first decision you need to make in planning a multipage publication. Either you can use one of the many sample designs that Publisher provides and customize it to meet your needs, or you can start from scratch. No matter which option you choose, you need to decide up front how many columns of text the publication will have, as well how many pages, it will be. You also need to decide how you want it to look when printed. For example, will the pages be folded or printed back to back? Karen uses the same newsletter design for each issue of *LoftLife* so that all issues have the same look and feel. For this issue, Karen decides to change the layout of the inside pages of the newsletter from three columns to two. As in the last issue, the pages will not be folded but will be printed back to back.

▶ What text to include and how to present it

Once you've chosen your layout, you then need to decide on your content. Write a list of all the articles you plan on including, like the one Karen created in the first column of Figure B-1. Then decide how you want to present your content. In a publication you can present text in two ways—either as a story or as a table. A **story**, also called an article, is comprised of text and is meant to be read from beginning to end. A **table** contains text or numbers in columns and rows. Use tables to organize information so that it is easy to read at a glance, such as the table of contents. Karen lists all the stories the *LoftLife* Editorial board picked for this issue.

▶ Where to place your text

Next, you have to plan where to place each story and table in the publication. Sometimes, all the text for a particular story won't fit in one text box, and needs to continue into another text box in a different part of the publication. This type of text is called **overflow text**. In the plan in Figure B-1, Karen notes that she needs to use overflow text for the Common Review Date story on page 1; she plans to continue it on page 4.

▶ What pictures and captions to include

Once you've settled on your stories, it's time to plan for graphics. A **picture caption** is a description that appears adjacent to a picture. When you add a picture or any object to your publication, you can choose to have Publisher wrap the text around that object or around the object's frame. **Wrapping** means that the text flows around the object rather than over it. Karen plans to wrap text around graphics for four stories in the newsletter.

▶ What content should appear on every page

A **header** is information that appears at the top of every page in your publication. A **footer** is information that appears at the bottom of every page in your publication. Karen will put the Volume and Issue number in the header of the newsletter, and will add a footer containing page numbers. She will specify not to show the header and footer on page 1.

▶ What special effects to include

Publisher gives you many tools to create special effects. For example, you can add **WordArt**—text that Publisher treats as a graphic. You can also add a pull quote or sidebar. A **pull quote** is a quotation from an article that is pulled out and treated like a graphic. A **sidebar** is text that is set apart from the major text but in some way relates to that text. You can also create unique effects by layering objects on top of each other to add depth and dimension to your publication. Figure B-2 shows the first page of the completed newsletter.

FIGURE B-1: Karen's content, layout, and graphics plan for the March issue of *LoftLife*

Stories for March issue →

Requires over-flow text →

Stories	Page	Contributor	Graphics
A Word from Our President	1	Leilani Ho	Insert pull-quote and wrap text around it; add Success graphic at end
Common Review Date	1, 4	Me	
Loftlife Needs You (sidebar)	1	Me	
Vision Service Plan	2	Jim Fernandez	Wrap text around Owl picture
401K Notes	2	John Kim	
Employee Advisory Resource	2	Me	Wrap text around EAR WordArt
Slaves to Fashion	3	Elizabeth Reed	Wrap text around pull quote between columns
They Asked for What?	4	Elizabeth Reed	

FIGURE B-2: Printout of page 1 of the completed newsletter

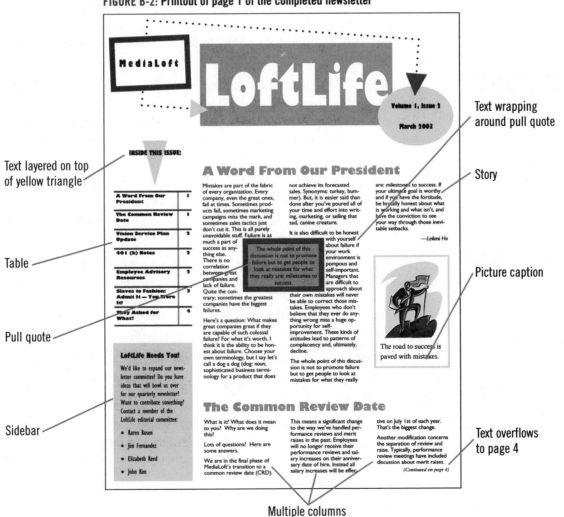

Text layered on top of yellow triangle

Table

Pull quote

Sidebar

Text wrapping around pull quote

Story

Picture caption

Text overflows to page 4

Multiple columns

Creating Columns of Text

Formatting text in columns can make text easier to read, and more visually appealing. To create columns, either you can choose a Publisher design that includes columns, or you can format text into columns using the options on the Newsletter Options task pane. Karen has been working on the newsletter for a few days. She used a Publisher sample design to create the newsletter, and then she replaced the placeholder text and graphics with the content for *LoftLife*. Today, she plans to finish the newsletter. She begins by opening the partially completed publication and changing the column format on the inside pages from three columns to two.

Steps

1. Start Publisher, then click the **More publications** link in the New Publication task pane
   The Open Publication dialog box opens.

2. Click the **Look in list arrow**, locate the drive and folder where your Project Files are stored, click **LoftLife.pub**, then click **Open**
   The newsletter opens with the first page displayed. Some graphic images are in the workspace below, which you will use later in the unit. The Mobile newsletter sample design with a three-column format was used to create the publication. The Page Navigation buttons indicate that the publication has four pages. The Newsletter Options task pane is open, with the two-sided printing and Customer Address/None options selected. You stick with these default options.

3. Click the **Page 2 Page Navigation button** on the status bar, click the **Zoom list arrow** on the Standard toolbar, then click **Whole Page**
   Pages 2 and 3 appear in the Publication window, as shown in Figure B-3. Pages 2 and 3 are a **two-page spread**. These are pages that will face each other when the publication is printed.

4. Click **Page Content** in the Newsletter Options task pane, then make sure **Left inside page** appears in the Select a page to modify text box
   See Figure B-4. The options on the task pane will apply to the left page because you have selected the Left inside page as the page to modify.

5. In the Columns on Left Page section in the task pane, click **2**
   Publisher reformats the left inside page with two columns. At this point, you could continue to change the content by choosing from the options under Content for Left Page in the task pane, but you are happy with the selected option of three stories. You see that Page 3 still has three columns, and looks odd next to the reformatted page 2.

6. Click the **Select a page to modify list arrow** in the Page Content task pane, click **Right inside page**, then click **2** in the Columns on Right Page section
   Page 3 now has two columns.

7. Close the task pane to view more of your workspace
   With the task pane closed, you can now see more of the newsletter. You can also see that there are graphic images in the workspace. You will add these to the newsletter later in the unit.

8. Save your changes to the newsletter

FIGURE B-3: Pages 2 and 3 of the newsletter

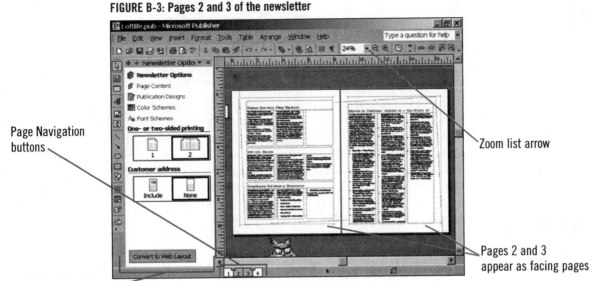

Page Navigation buttons

Zoom list arrow

Newsletter Options task pane

Pages 2 and 3 appear as facing pages

FIGURE B-4: Changing the number of columns with the Page Content task pane

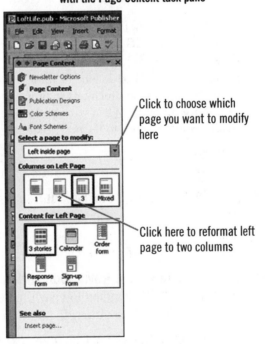

Click to choose which page you want to modify here

Click here to reformat left page to two columns

Creating columns in existing text boxes

You can also change the number of columns of text in existing text boxes. Sometimes it is easier to read narrower columns. For example, you could turn one wide column of text into two or three more readable columns. To create columns in an existing text box, right-click the text box, then click Format Text Box from the shortcut menu. Click the Text Box tab, click Columns to open the Columns dialog box, then specify the number of columns and the amount of spacing between the columns, as shown in Figure B-5.

FIGURE B-5: Columns dialog box

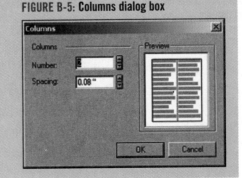

Working with Overflow Text

Sometimes there isn't enough room in a text box to hold all of the text for a particular story. When this happens, a Text in Overflow icon appears at the bottom of the text box to indicate that not all text in the story is visible. To display all the text, you either must enlarge the text box or continue the story in another text box in the publication. To continue a story in another text box, you connect that text box to the overflowing text box, and then "pour" the overflow text into the next text box. See Table B-1 for a description of the different text flow icons. Karen asked one of her colleagues to write a 500-word article for the newsletter on MediaLoft's new annual review policy. She plans to begin this story on page 1 and continue it on page 4. Karen receives the article as a Word file and imports it into the newsletter.

Steps 1234

QuickTip

Click [←→] to select the next frame.

1. **Click the Page 1 Page Navigation button, click the first column text box** beneath the headline "The Common Review Date" to select it, then press **[F9]**
   The Go to Next Frame icon [←→] indicates that the selected frame is linked to the text box in the next column, as shown in Figure B-6. These text boxes are **connected**.

2. **Click Insert on the menu bar, click Text File** to open the Insert Text dialog box, click the **Look in list arrow** to locate the drive and folder where your Project Files are stored, click **PB B-1.doc**, then click **OK**
   The text from the Word document automatically pours into the three connected text boxes on page 1, but there's too much text to fit in the three boxes, so a message appears asking if you want to use autoflow. When you use **Autoflow**, Publisher automatically flows text from one existing empty text box to the next, asking for confirmation before it flows into each text box.

3. **Click No**
   The Text in Overflow icon appears at the bottom of the text box.

4. **Click the Create Text Box Link button** 🔗 **on the Connect Frames toolbar**
   The pointer changes to a pitcher. When you place the pointer over a text box that doesn't include the current story, the pitcher changes to. When you click an empty text box with the pitcher pointer, the overflow text flows into that text box.

QuickTip

You can press [Ctrl][G], enter a page number, then click OK to move to another page in your publication.

5. **Click the Page 4 Page Navigation button,** then click the **first column text box** under the headline "The Common Review Date (continued)"
   Again, the text does not entirely fit in the text box, as shown in Figure B-7.

6. **Click** 🔗, click the **second column text box**, click 🔗 then click the **third column text box**

QuickTip

If you add pages to a publication, Continued on page numbers are automatically updated.

7. **Go to page 1**, right-click the **third column text box** of the story, click **Format Text Box** on the shortcut menu, then click the **Text Box tab**
   See Figure B-8. **Continued notices** provide a roadmap. If a story continues on another page, these cues help the reader find the rest of the story.

8. **Click the Include "Continued on page…" check box** to select it, then click **OK**
   Publisher adds the text "(Continued on page 4)" to the bottom of the text box.

9. **Go to page 4**, right-click the **first column text box** of the story, click **Format Text Box**, click the **Text Box tab**, click the **Include "Continued from page…" checkbox** to select it, click **OK**, then save your work

FIGURE B-6: Two connected text boxes

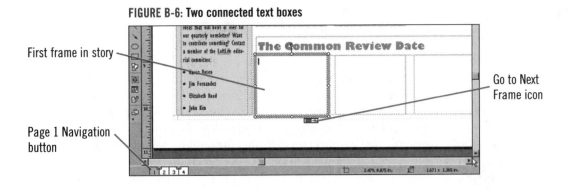

First frame in story

Go to Next Frame icon

Page 1 Navigation button

FIGURE B-7: Connecting text from one frame to another

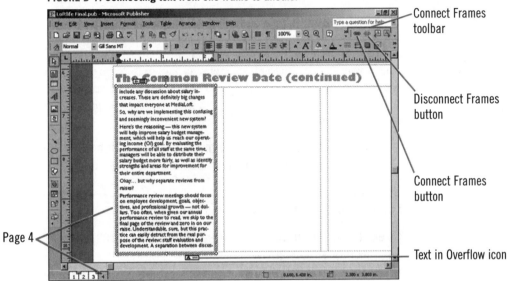

Connect Frames toolbar

Disconnect Frames button

Connect Frames button

Page 4

Text in Overflow icon

FIGURE B-8: Format Text Box dialog box with Text Box tab displayed

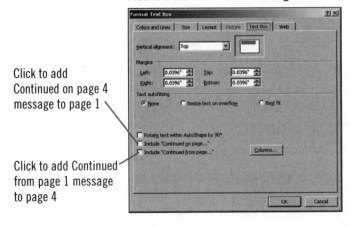

Click to add Continued on page 4 message to page 1

Click to add Continued from page 1 message to page 4

TABLE B-1: Text Flow icons

text flow icon	description
← ▭	Indicates that text box is connected to another text box and that text flows from that text box to this one. Click to quickly move to the previous frame.
▭ →	Indicates that text box is connected to another text box and that text flows to that text box. Click to quickly move to the next frame.
A •••	Indicates that text box is not connected to another text box and that there is more text that does not fit in the text frame.

Using Guides

When you are working with columns, it can be helpful to use layout and ruler guides. **Layout guides** are nonprinting lines that help you to align text, pictures, and other objects into columns and rows so that your publication will have a consistent look across all pages. Layout guides appear on every page of your publication and are represented by blue and pink dotted lines on the screen. **Ruler guides** are similar to layout guides but appear only on a single page. Use ruler guides whenever you need a little extra help aligning an object on a page. Ruler guides are represented by green dotted lines on the screen. Karen notices that the column containing the table of contents and sidebar on page 1 is not the same width as the other columns on the page. Setting vertical layout guides will help her to fix this. She inserts a ruler guide to help position a picture.

Steps

1. Go to **page 1**, click the **Zoom list arrow**, click **Whole Page**, click **Arrange** on the menu bar, then click **Layout Guides**

   The Layout Guides dialog box opens, as shown in Figure B-9. Use this dialog box to adjust the margin guides and grid guides. The margin guides appear in pink on screen and outline the **margin**, or perimeter, of the page. The grid guides appear in blue on screen and provide a perimeter for each column on the page.

2. Click the **Columns up arrow** to display 4 in the Number of Columns text box

   The Preview shows blue grid guides dividing the page into four columns.

3. Click **OK**

   Layout guides appear on the newsletter.

4. Select the **table of contents table frame**, then press **[F9]** to zoom in on that frame, as shown in Figure B-10

   If you carefully position the pointer over a sizing handle on the vertical border of a column in the table, the pointer ◀▌▶ and a ScreenTip that says "Table Frame" appear, allowing you to adjust the width of the column. If you place the pointer on a sizing handle on the horizontal border the ⬍ pointer appears to allow you to adjust the height of the row.

5. Point to the **sizing handle on the right border** of the table, drag ◀▌▶ to the left to align the right edge of the table frame with the blue grid guide, then click outside the frame to check your work

   The table of contents table frame is now the same width as the grid guide.

QuickTip

To clear all ruler guides, click Arrange on the menu bar, point to Ruler Guides, then click Clear all Ruler Guides.

6. Scroll down and click the **yellow sidebar LoftLife Needs You! text box**, drag the **middle-right handle** to the left to align with the blue grid guide, then click outside the text box to check your work

   Both frames in the first column have been resized.

7. Scroll up to view the "A Word From..." story, click **Arrange** on the menu bar, point to **Ruler Guides**, then click **Add Horizontal Ruler Guide**

   A green horizontal line appears on the page.

8. Place the pointer over the green line, press and hold **[Shift]** so the pointer changes to the Adjust pointer ⬍ click and drag ⬍ to align with the 5½" mark on the vertical ruler, then release **[Shift]**

   The ruler guide is now set as shown in Figure B-11. You will use this newly created ruler guide in the next lesson.

9. Save your changes

FIGURE B-9: Layout Guides dialog box

Margin Guides section
Number of Columns
Number of Rows
Grid Guides section

Preview guides

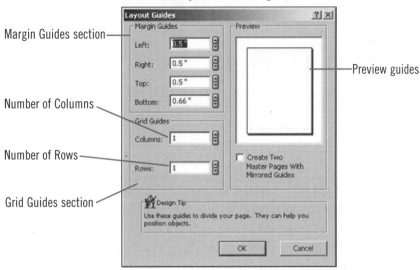

FIGURE B-10: Table of contents table frame

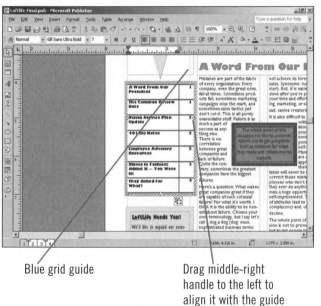

Blue grid guide

Drag middle-right handle to the left to align it with the guide

FIGURE B-11: Setting a ruler guide

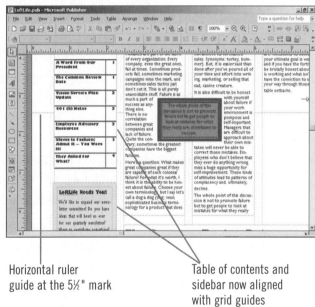

Horizontal ruler guide at the 5½" mark

Table of contents and sidebar now aligned with grid guides

Clues to Use

Aligning objects

You can align objects with guides by hand or you can have Publisher align them for you. To align an object by hand, simply drag or resize the object using the mouse. The Object Position and Object Size indicators in the status bar can help you to place objects exactly. You can also use Publisher's Snap to and Nudge features to help you align objects precisely to guides. To turn on the Snap to feature, enable one or more of the Snap to commands on the Arrange menu. Snap to Ruler Marks snaps an object to the closest ruler mark, Snap to Guides automatically snaps an object to the closest layout guide, and Snap to Objects snaps an object to the closest object. Publisher's Nudge feature allows you to move or "nudge" an object one small increment at a time. To nudge an object, select the object, click Arrange on the menu bar, click Nudge, then click Up, Down, Left, or Right. You can also nudge an object by pressing and holding [Alt] while pressing one of the arrow keys.

Publisher 2002

Creating Picture Captions

A **picture caption** is text that describes or elaborates on a picture. Captions can be located above, below, or next to a picture. You can create a picture caption by typing text in a text box that you create, or you can use Publisher's Design Gallery to choose one of the picture caption designs. The design collection includes objects such as picture captions, logos, and calendars. The designs are organized by category and design type. You can also create and save your own objects in the Design Gallery.　　　　Karen would like to add an inspirational piece of clip art at the bottom of the president's article on page 1. She does this by using one of Publisher's pre-set picture captions in the Design Gallery and choosing an appropriate piece of clip art.

1. On page 1, select the **first column text box** below the "A Word From Our President" text box, then press **[F9]** to zoom in on the article, if necessary

2. Click the **Design Gallery Object button** 🖼 on the Objects toolbar
   The Microsoft Publisher Design Gallery opens, as shown in Figure B-12. Each of the three tabs has a list of categories or design sets. The Categories list in the left pane shows the large variety of types of predesigned objects you can use to enhance your publications. The right pane shows thumbnails of the selected category you can insert in the publication.

3. On the Objects by Category tab, click **Picture Captions** in the Categories list, click the **Thin Frame Picture Caption**, then click **Insert Object**
   The object, an image with "Caption describing picture or graphic" text appears on top of the article.

4. Scroll to view the bottom of the third column of that story, then drag the **object** using the Move Pointer 🖑 so that the upper-left handle of the object is positioned at the intersection of the ruler guide and the layout guide, as shown in Figure B-13

5. Drag the **lower-right handle** up and to the left using the Resize Pointer ⬉ to resize the frame so that it is aligned with the bottom of the column at the 7⅞" mark on the vertical ruler and the right layout guide
   The Design Gallery provides a placeholder graphic as well as placeholder caption text. You can change it at any time.

Trouble?

If a dialog box opens asking if you want to catalog all the images on your hard drive for the Media Gallery, click Later.

6. Click the **picture of the coffee cup,** handles appear around the picture when it is selected, right click the **picture,** point to **Change Picture** on the shortcut menu, then click **Clip Art**
   The Insert Clip Art Task pane opens.

7. Type **success** in the Search text text box, click **Search**, then scroll down the results to display the **picture of a man holding a flag on a mountain top**, as shown in Figure B-14
   The Insert Clip Art task pane displays the results of your search. If you click the right side of any image a menu appears with various options for working with the image in the Clip Organizer.

Trouble?

If you don't see this picture click another image.

8. Click the **picture of a man holding a flag on a mountain top** to insert it, click the **placeholder caption text** to select it, type **The road to success is paved with mistakes.**, then click outside the object
   The placeholder picture and caption are replaced with a relevant image and text.

9. Close the Clip Art task pane, then save your changes

FIGURE B-12: Microsoft Publisher Design Gallery

Objects by
Category tab

Your Objects tab

Categories of
Publisher-designed
objects

Objects by Design tab

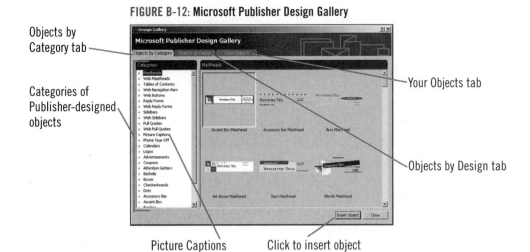

Picture Captions

Click to insert object

FIGURE B-13: Positioning the object using guides

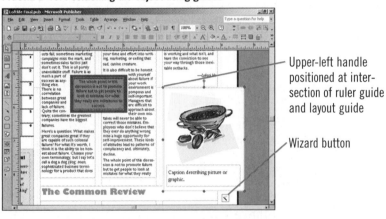

Upper-left handle
positioned at inter-
section of ruler guide
and layout guide

Wizard button

FIGURE B-14: Inserting Clip Art using the task pane

Search results for
"success"

Click to insert this
image into the
newsletter

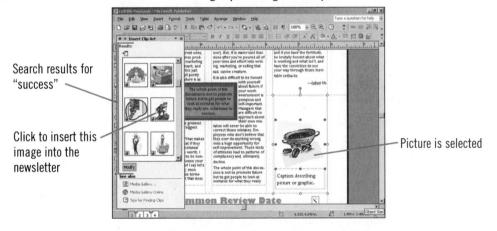

Picture is selected

CLUES TO USE

Adding your own objects to the Design Gallery

You can add your own objects to the Design Gallery for use in future publications. For example, if you design your own pull quote that you intend to use in every edition of an annual publication, you would want to add this to the Design Gallery. Select the object you want to save, click Insert on the menu bar, and then click Add Selection to Design Gallery. In the Add Object dialog box, type a name for the object and type or choose a category, then click OK. This object will then appear on the Your Objects tab. To delete an object from the Your Objects tab of the Design Gallery, right-click the object, click Delete This Object on the shortcut menu, then click Yes to confirm the deletion.

Creating Headers and Footers

A **header** is information that appears on the top of every page of a publication, such as the name of the publication. A **footer** is information that appears on the bottom of every page of a publication, such as a page number. When you create a header or footer in Publisher, you use the Header and Footer command on the View menu. When you choose the Header and Footer command, Publisher opens the **master page**, also known as the **background**, which is a layer that appears behind every page in a publication. The **foreground** sits on top of the background and consists of the objects that appear on a specific page of a publication. Karen adds a header and a footer to her newsletter. She does not want them to appear on page 1.

1. Click **View** on the menu bar, click **Header and Footer**, then press **[F9]** to zoom out
   The background right master page appears, showing an empty text box at the top of the page for a header and one at the bottom for a footer. The Header and Footer toolbar is also open. At the moment, the page navigation buttons show an "R," indicating that there is only one master page, which by default is the right-hand one. Because this publication has two-page spreads, you need both a right and a left master page, which will be mirror images of each other.

2. Click **Arrange** on the menu bar, click **Layout Guides**, click the **Create Two Master Pages With Mirrored Guides** check box, then click **OK**
   Before entering text in the header text box, you need to make sure that both header text boxes and both footer text boxes are correctly aligned with the blue layout guides.

3. If necessary, drag header text box and each footer text box to the position shown in Figure B-15

4. Click in the **left page Header text box**, press **[F9]** to zoom in, type **VOLUME 1 ISSUE 2**, then click the **Align Right button** on the Formatting toolbar

5. Scroll over to the right page, click in the **right page Header text box**, then type **VOLUME 1 ISSUE 2**
   The right header text is left-aligned by default. Compare your publication with Figure B-16.

6. Click the **Show Header/Footer button** on the Header and Footer toolbar to move the insertion point to the right-page footer, type **Page**, press **[Spacebar]**, click the **Insert Page Number button** on the Header and Footer toolbar, then click
   A yellow box appears, explaining that Publisher will automatically insert a page number. The page number will be right-aligned in the footer on the right page.

7. Select **Page #**, click the **Copy button** on the Standard toolbar, scroll over to the left page, click in the **footer text box**, then click the **Paste button**
   The footer text from the right page is copied to the left footer. See Figure B-17.

8. Press **[Ctrl][M]**, then use the Page Navigation buttons to view all pages of your publication
   You can see both headers and footers on each page.

9. Go to page 1, click **View** on the menu bar, then click **Ignore Master Page**
   The header and footer no longer appear on page 1 but still appear on pages 2–4.

FIGURE B-15: Left and right master pages

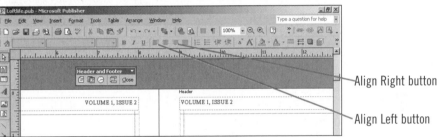

Header and footer toolbar

Empty footer text boxes

Left and right master page navigation buttons

Empty header text boxes

Left and right master pages

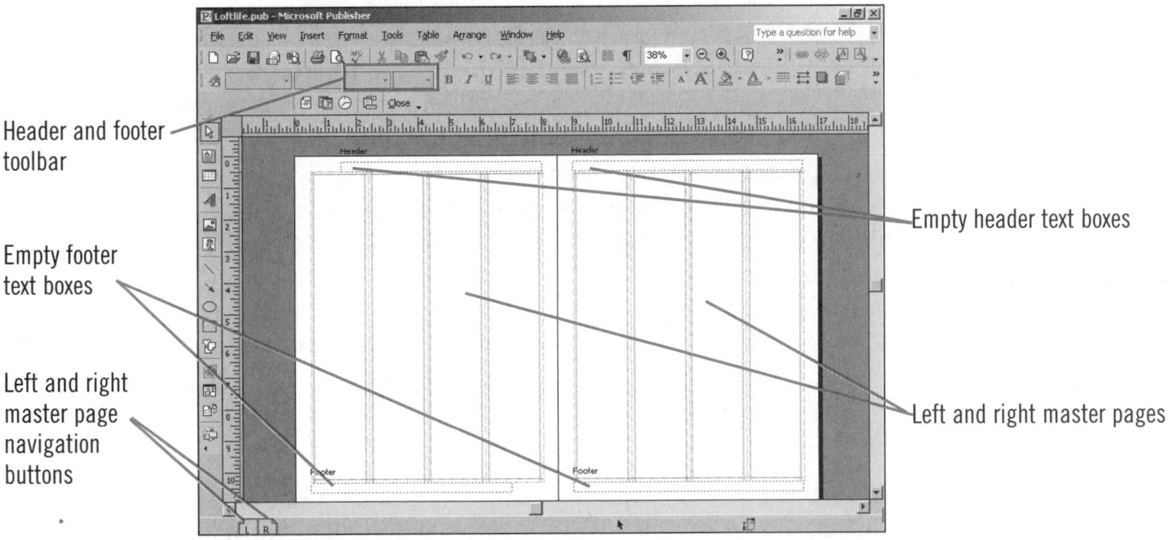

FIGURE B-16: Completed headers

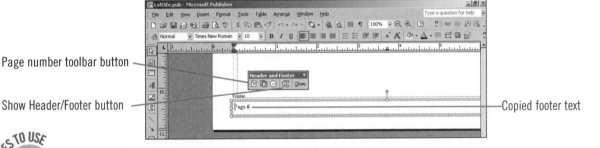

Align Right button

Align Left button

FIGURE B-17: Completed left page footer

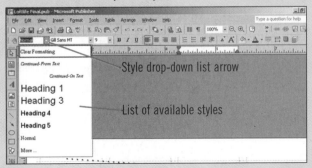

Page number toolbar button

Show Header/Footer button

Copied footer text

CLUES TO USE

Working with text styles

A text style is a set of formatting characteristics that you can quickly apply to text on a paragraph-by-paragraph basis. A style contains all text formatting information: font and font size, font color, alignment, indents, character and line spacing, tabs, and special formatting, such as numbered lists. Publisher includes preset styles that you can apply, or you can import text styles from other publications or define your own styles. To apply a text style, select the text you want to format, click the Style list arrow on the Formatting toolbar, as shown in Figure B-18, and then choose from the list of styles. To modify a style or create a new style, use the Styles and Formatting command on the

Formatting menu to open the Styles and Formatting task pane.

FIGURE B-18: Publisher preset styles

Style drop-down list arrow

List of available styles

Publisher 2002

Inserting and Formatting WordArt

WordArt is text that Publisher treats as a graphic. You click the Insert Word Art button on the Objects toolbar to choose one of the preset designs, you enter the text that you want to create as art, then you use the many formatting options available on the WordArt toolbar to curve, stretch, and twist the text. WordArt is a fun way to add color and style to your publications. The Employee Advisory Resource article is all text with no graphics. Karen decides to create WordArt out of the letters EAR to make the article more appealing to read.

Steps

1. Go to **page 2**, scroll so that the Employee Advisory Resource story is in view, then click in the **desktop workspace** so that no frames are selected in the newsletter

2. Click the **Insert WordArt button** on the Objects toolbar
   The WordArt Gallery dialog box opens, displaying 30 preset styles for WordArt.

3. Click the **blue curved design in the fourth row**, as shown in Figure B-19, then click **OK**
   The Edit WordArt dialog box opens. This is where you enter the text and specify the font, the font size, and whether the text is bold or italic.

4. Type **EAR** in the text box, click the **Font list arrow**, click **Ravie**, click the **Size list arrow**, click **40**, then click **OK**
   The WordArt appears selected on your publication, and the WordArt toolbar is open. You can use this toolbar to make additional formatting changes to the WordArt. First you need to position the WordArt in the Employee Advisory Resource story.

5. Drag the **EAR** WordArt until it is positioned between the two columns of text in the middle of the Employee Advisory Resource story
   Notice that the text in the story automatically wraps around the WordArt. Wrapping is explored in the next lesson.

6. Click the **Format WordArt button** on the WordArt toolbar
   The Format WordArt dialog box opens, as shown in Figure B-20. You can use this dialog box to change the lines, borders, colors, size, and layout of your WordArt.

7. Click the **Fill Color list arrow** on the Colors and Lines tab, click **the yellow square**, click the **Line Color list arrow**, click **the red square**, click the **Line Dashed list arrow**, click the **Square Dot pattern**, then click **OK**
   The EAR WordArt now appears with the formatting changes you made.

8. Click the **WordArt Shape button** on the WordArt toolbar, then click the **Can Up shape** in the third row, third column
   The EAR WordArt now appears with a new shape. You can always drag a handle on the selected WordArt to change the existing shape if you want.

9. Close the Word Art toolbar, then save your changes to the newsletter
   The WordArt you created looks great! See Figure B-21.

FIGURE B-19: WordArt Gallery dialog box

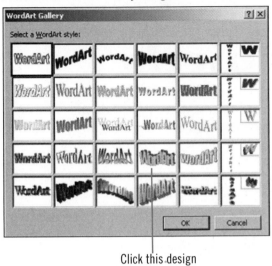

Click this design

Figure B-20: Format WordArt dialog box

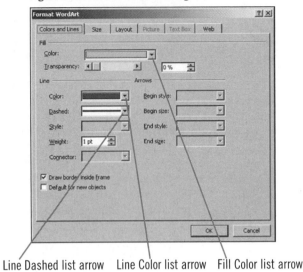

Line Dashed list arrow   Line Color list arrow   Fill Color list arrow

FIGURE B-21: Completed WordArt

Newly created WordArt

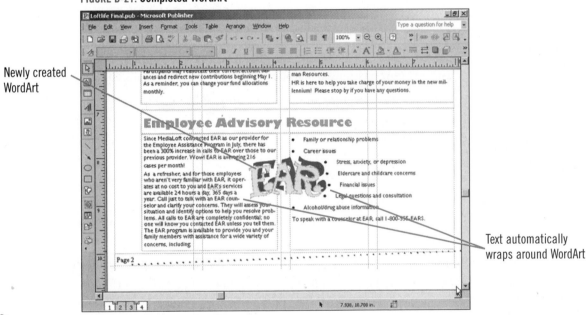

Text automatically wraps around WordArt

Creating a drop cap

A drop cap is a specially formatted first letter of the first word of a paragraph. Usually, a drop cap is in a much larger font size than the paragraph text itself, and sometimes the drop cap is formatted in a different font. To create a drop cap, click anywhere in the paragraph where you want the drop cap to appear, click Format on the menu bar, click Drop Cap, click one of the available drop cap styles in the Drop Cap dialog box, shown in Figure B-22, then click OK. You can also use the options on the Custom Drop Cap tab to create your own drop cap style.

FIGURE B-22: Drop Cap dialog box

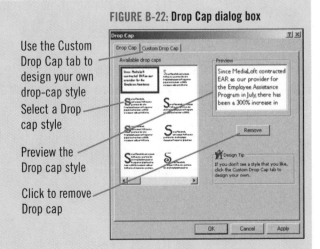

Use the Custom Drop Cap tab to design your own drop-cap style

Select a Drop cap style

Preview the Drop cap style

Click to remove Drop cap

Wrapping Text Around Objects

To help make your stories more visually interesting, Publisher gives you the ability to wrap text around any object. **Wrapping** means that the text flows around the object rather than on top of or behind it. You can wrap text around pictures or around other text, such as pull quotes. A **pull quote** is a quotation from a story that is pulled out into its own frame and treated like a graphic. You can choose to wrap text around an object's frame or around the object itself. Karen is ready to add graphics to her stories on page 2 and 3. She collected graphics and placed them on the workspace. She plans to place an owl graphic in the Vision Service story on page 2, and will insert a pull quote into the Fashion story on page 3. She will wrap text around both objects.

Steps 1 2 3 4

1. Go to page 2, zoom out to view the whole page if necessary
   You can store clip art in the desktop workspace for use in the publication.

2. Drag the **owl clip art** located at the bottom of your desktop workspace so that it is centered in between the two columns of text in the "Vision Service Plan Update" story, click **Arrange** on the menu bar, point to **Order**, then click **Bring to Front**
   The text in the article automatically wraps around the square-shaped frame containing the owl.

3. Click **Arrange** on the menu bar, point to **Text Wrapping**, then click **Tight**
   The text now wraps tightly around the contours of the owl's body.

4. Click **Insert** on the menu bar, click **Design Gallery Object**, then click **Pull Quotes** in the Categories list
   The Design Gallery opens, with the Objects by Category tab and Pull Quotes selected, as shown in Figure B-23.

5. Scroll down the Pull Quotes in the right pane, click the **Mobile Pull Quote** design, then click **Insert Object**
   The pull quote frame with placeholder text is now positioned in the middle of the two-page spread, between page 2 and 3.

6. Drag the **Pull Quote frame** to the "Slaves to Fashion" story so that it is centered between the two columns at the 4" mark on the vertical ruler
   Notice that the text automatically wraps around the pull quote frame.

7. Zoom in on the lower-right corner of page 3, drag to select the last bulleted item in the second column, beginning with In junior high…, including Paul Roudenko, then click the **Copy button** 🖺 on the Standard toolbar
   Text can be copied from one text box or frame to another.

8. Scroll to view the Pull quote box, click to select the **placeholder text**, then click the **Paste button** 🖺 on the Standard toolbar
   The quote from Paul Roudenko is pulled out and highlighted in the pull quote on the page.

9. Select all the text in the pull quote, click the **Font list arrow** on the Formatting toolbar, click **Times New Roman**, click the **Size list arrow**, click **10**, click the **Italic button** 𝐼 on the Formatting toolbar, then save your changes
   Compare your publication with Figure B-24.

FIGURE B-23: Design Gallery with Pull Quotes category selected

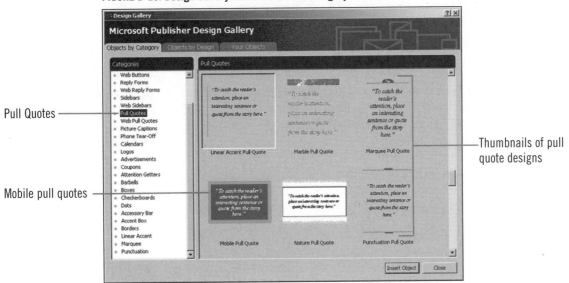

Pull Quotes

Mobile pull quotes

Thumbnails of pull quote designs

FIGURE B-24: Wrapping text around clip art and pull quotes

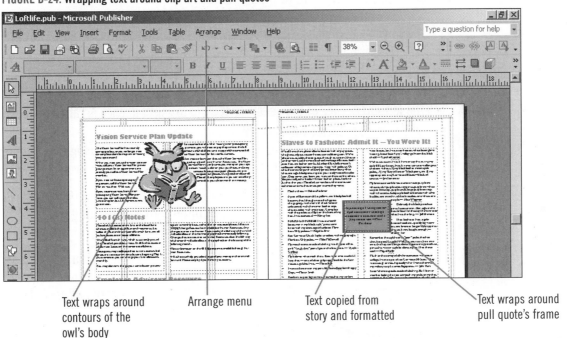

Text wraps around contours of the owl's body

Arrange menu

Text copied from story and formatted

Text wraps around pull quote's frame

CLUES TO USE

Rotating and flipping objects

You can create interesting effects in a publication by rotating or flipping text and objects. When you rotate an object, you change its angle in degrees relative to a baseline. For example, text that is rotated 90 degrees appears vertically rather than horizontally. To rotate an object in 90-degree increments, select the object, click Arrange on the menu bar, point to Rotate of Flip, then click the option you want. To rotate an object by dragging it, select the object, then point to the green rotation handle at the top of the frame. Drag the mouse in the direction you want to rotate. To rotate the object in 15-degree increments using the dragging method, press and hold [Shift] while dragging the rotation handle.

Layering and Grouping Objects

You can layer two or more objects on top of each other in a publication to create an interesting visual effect. When you layer objects, they appear on the page in the order you placed them, as if you had placed different pieces of paper on top of one another. You can change the layer order by using the Bring to Front, Send to Back, Bring Forward, or Send Backward commands. When you are happy with the arrangement of your layered objects, you can **group** them so you can work with the objects as a single object. Grouping objects allows you to move and resize the group rather than each object individually, saving time. ✎ Karen wants to improve the look of the MediaLoft contact information on page 4 of *LoftLife*. She decides to layer the logo on top of several different rectangle shapes to make it more attractive.

Steps 1 2 3 4

1. Go to **page 4**, then zoom in on the upper-left corner of the page and the desktop workspace to the left of the page
   The MediaLoft logo is positioned above the yellow box, and an autoshape graphic with a blue border is seen in the desktop workspace. An **autoshape** is a predesigned shape provided with Publisher that you can use in your publications.

2. Select the **blue-bordered rectangle** in the desktop workspace, then drag it to the publication page so that the upper-left corner is positioned at the 1" marks on both the horizontal and vertical rulers
   Compare your screen to Figure B-25.

3. Click the **top-left corner of the yellow rectangle** to select it, click **Arrange** on the menu bar, point to **Order**, then click **Send to Back**
   The yellow rectangle is now positioned behind the blue-bordered rectangle. Once you perform an Order operation, an order button will appear on the Standard toolbar with a list arrow.

4. Click the **logo**, click the **Bring to Front button** 🔲 on the Standard toolbar, then drag the logo down so that it is centered in the blue-bordered rectangle
   The logo is now on top of the blue-edged rectangle, which is on top of the yellow rectangle.

5. Click the **logo**, press and hold [Shift], then click the **blue-bordered rectangle**
   Notice that both of the frames are selected and the Group Objects button 🔲 appears in the lower-right corner of the selection box. Clicking this button groups all the selected objects into one single object.

6. Click the **Group Objects button** 🔲
   The objects are now all grouped and you can move, resize, or format them as a whole, as shown in Figure B-26. The Group Objects button has changed to an Ungroup Objects button 🔲 now that the selected object is a group. You can click this button to ungroup the objects and work with them individually.

7. Select **Tel: (415) 555-2398** in the yellow rectangle, type **your name**, press [Enter], type **Editor**, then save your changes to the newsletter

8. Click the **Spell check button** 🔲 on the Standard toolbar, check all the stories in the publication, correct any misspelled words, save any changes, then print the newsletter

9. Compare your newsletter to Figure B-27

FIGURE B-25: **Working with three layers**

Bring to Front button

Logo

Blue-bordered rectangle

Yellow rectangle

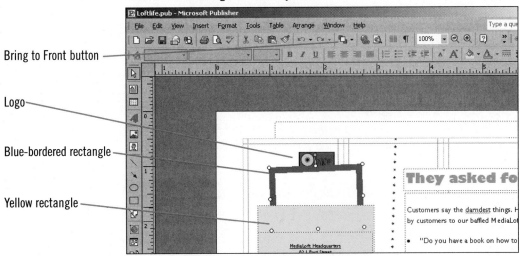

FIGURE B-26: **Grouping objects**

Both objects are selected as a group

Ungroup Objects button

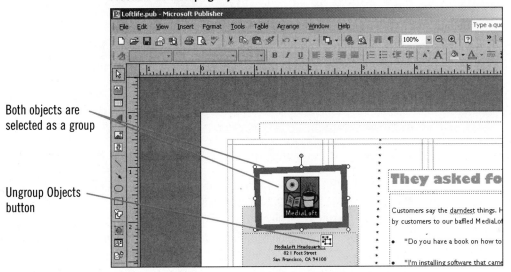

FIGURE B-27: **Completed newsletter**

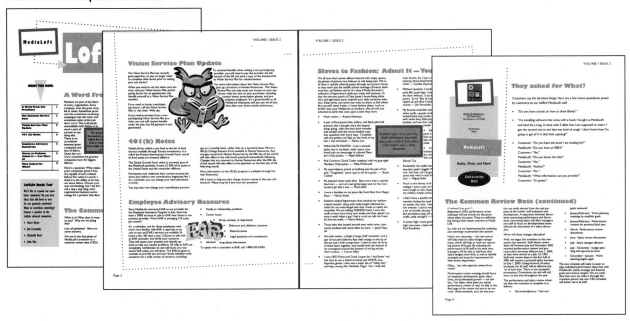

Practice

► Concepts Review

Label each element of the publication shown in Figure B-28.

FIGURE B-28

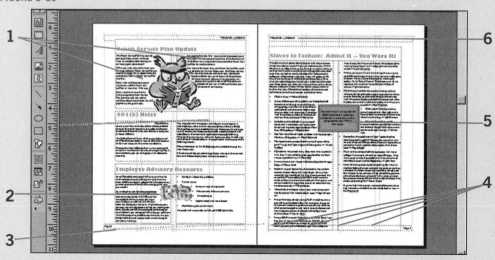

Match each term with the statement that best describes it.

7. **Ruler guides**
8. **Foreground**
9. **Autoflow**
10. **Send to Back**
11. **Story**
12. **Layout guides**
13. **Master page**
14. **Header**

a. Also called an article, is comprised of text and meant to be read from top to bottom
b. Feature that flows text from one text box to another
c. The layer where you place objects that you want to appear on every page
d. The layer where you place objects that you want to appear on individual pages
e. Command used to send an object behind of a stack of objects
f. Nonprinting lines that can assist you in aligning objects on individual pages
g. Information that appears at the top of every page of a publication
h. Nonprinting lines that can assist you in aligning objects on all pages

► Skills Review

1. **Create columns of text.**
   a. Start Publisher, open the file Rental.pub, then go to page 2 of the publication.
   b. Right-click the text box beneath the heading "Why Rent a Computer", then change the number of columns in this text box to **2**, with **.14"** of space in between then close the Format Text Box dialog box.

2. **Work with overflow text.**
   a. Select the empty text box in the second panel on page 2, insert the file PB B-2.doc into it, then click No when asked if you want to use autoflow.
   b. Connect the text box containing PB B-2 to the empty text box in the third panel on page 2, then insert the overflow text into this connected text box.
   c. Connect the text box in the third column of page 2 to the blue text box in the first column of page 1.
   d. Go to page 2. Insert a Continued on notice at the end of the text box in the third panel on page 2, then insert a Continued from notice at the beginning of the text box in the first panel on page 1.

3. Use guides.

   a. Create layout guides for three columns.

   b. In the first panel on page 2, increase the width of the text box containing the double columns of text so that both sides of the text box are aligned with the blue layout guides.

   c. Drag the bottom middle handle of the text box up to the 5 ½" mark on the vertical ruler.

4. Create picture captions.

   a. In the Why Rent a Computer? panel, insert a picture caption below the text box. Choose the Box Picture design.

   b. Resize and move the picture so that its top edge is just below the text, and its bottom edge is at the 8" mark on the vertical ruler.

   c. Replace the placeholder graphic with a picture of a computer from the Insert Clip Art task pane, then replace the placeholder caption text with **Why buy when you can rent?**

   d. Change the font of the picture caption to 9 pt Rockwell Condensed.

5. Create headers and footers.

   a. Insert a header at the top of the first column that contains this text: **Visit us at www.qcrental.com!**

   b. Insert a footer at the bottom of the first column that contains this text: **Call Quality Computer today at (314) 555-1000!**

   c. Verify that the footer and header text is left-aligned, format the footer and header text in Rockwell 10 point italic, then close the Header and Footer toolbar.

6. Insert and format WordArt.

   a. Go to page 1, then open the WordArt Gallery.

   b. Choose the WordArt Style that is in the second row, fifth column of the WordArt Gallery.

   c. Type **the computer experts** in the text box, and choose Bodoni MT Black 20 point bold for the font.

   d. Position the WordArt frame so that it is centered in the middle panel with the top of the WordArt frame at the 1" mark on the vertical ruler.

   e. Format the WordArt with the Wave 1 shape (third row, fifth column), change the fill color to orange and the line color to dark blue, then close the WordArt toolbar.

7. Wrap text around objects.

   a. Go to page 1, select the computer clip art from the bottom of the first column and move it up into the paragraph of text, so its top edge is at the 3" mark on the vertical ruler and its left edge is flush against the text box. Choose the square text wrapping option.

   b. Go to the story in the first panel of page 2, then insert a pull quote using the Arcs Pull Quote design.

   c. Position the pull quote frame so that it is centered between the two columns of text in the first panel, with the top edge at the 3" mark on the vertical ruler.

   d. Replace the placeholder text with **As soon as you buy a system, it is outdated**. Resize the pull quote frame by dragging the bottom-middle handle up to the 4" mark on the vertical ruler, then format the text in Rockwell 9 point italic.

8. Layer and group objects.

   a. In the workspace to the right of the brochure, create the Quality Computer logo by assembling the Quality Computer, Inc. text with the red rectangle, the dot pattern, the black square, and the black-bordered shape. Use the logo at the top of page 1 as a model, using the red rectangle in place of the blue.

   b. Use the Order buttons as necessary to complete this task. When the logo is assembled correctly, group the items and move the logo to just above the address on page 2.

c. Go to page 1, then create a text box at the 5" mark on the vertical ruler of the middle panel, that is approximately 1/2" high and spanning the width of the column, then type your name in the text box and format the font as 14 pt Rockwell. Center-align the text.

d. Proofread and spell check all stories, save your changes, print and close the publication, then exit Publisher.

▶ Independent Challenge 1

You are a travel agent with Escape Travel. You are in charge of creating a brochure on vacations to Nova Scotia. Several colleagues have e-mailed you marketing text to include in the brochure. You started your brochure a few days ago and now need to add the finishing touches.

a. Start Publisher, open the file Nova Scotia.pub, then add layout guides for three columns.

b. On page 2, insert the Project File PB B-3.doc into the two empty columns. Do not use autoflow.

c. Insert a picture caption under Nova Scotia in the third column of page 1. Choose a picture frame that you like and change the placeholder text to **Get away today!** Format the caption text in 14 point Franklin Gothic Demi. Replace the picture with a map of Nova Scotia from the Insert Clip Art task pane.

d. Insert a right-aligned footer with the text **Call Escape Travel at (207) 555-1234 for more information**, then create a left-aligned header that contains your name.

e. Create WordArt in the second column on page 1 with the text **Nova Scotia**. Format the WordArt with any shape, font, and colors that you choose, then proofread, spell check, save, and print the publication.

▶ Independent Challenge 2

You are the development director for the Wolf Pond Arts Academy. You have partially completed a brochure announcing the annual fundraiser. You need to finish placing objects and formatting it.

a. Start Publisher, and open the file **Fundraiser.pub**.

b. In the third panel on page 1, replace the text <name> in the 2 text boxes with **Wolf Pond Arts Academy**.

c. In the leftmost panel on page 1, replace the text Back panel heading with **Live Onstage**. In the text box below this heading, insert two pieces of clip art that illustrate the paragraph text. Resize the graphics to appropriate sizes, and specify the text wrapping of your choice.

d. In the first panel on page 2, insert PB B-4.doc in the text box below "Our annual fundraising gala!" increase the size of the text box by aligning the right edge with the layout guide, then format the text into two columns.

e. Insert any pull quote centered between the two columns of text. Use the Carla Davis quote from the paragraph, and format the text in Times New Roman 9 point italic. Reduce the size of the pull quote box to 1" tall by 1" wide.

f. Create WordArt for **WPAA**, and insert it in the space above the address on the second panel of page 1.

g. In the top text box in the middle panel on page 1, replace the text <designer> with your name, proofread, spell check, save, print and close the publication.

▶ Independent Challenge 3

You've written a few pages of text outlining methods for improving food access in your community. Now, you want to print and distribute what you've written as a pamphlet, as four pages on a folded sheet of paper.

a. Start Publisher, open a new blank publication, then save the publication as **Food Recovery**.

b. Click File on the menu bar, open the Page Setup dialog box, choose Booklet in the Publication type list box, choose Portrait for the Orientation, click OK, then click Yes in the dialog box that asks if you want to automatically insert pages.

c. On page 1 of the publication, insert a text box that aligns with the left, right, and bottom layout guides, and begins at the 5" mark on the vertical ruler.

d. Add text boxes to pages 2, 3, and 4 that occupy all the space within the blue layout guides.

e. Connect the text box from page 1 to page 2, connect the text box from page 2 to page 3, and then connect the text box from page 3 to page 4.

f. Insert the text from the file PB B-5.doc, beginning in the text box on page 1. Click No if asked about Autoflow. Pour the text to all four pages.

g. Add a text box to the top of page 1, and enter an appropriate title, along with your name as the author.

h. Format the first letter of the first paragraph of the essay as a drop cap. (*Hint:* See clues on page B-15.)

i Create a pull quote of your own choice on page 2 or 3 of the publication.

j. Proofread and spell check, save the publication, print, close it, then exit Publisher.

Independent Challenge 4

You own a small bed and breakfast in a city of your choice, anywhere in the world. You decide to create a brochure to attract visitors to your inn. You first need to do some research on the Internet about your chosen city.

a. Log on to the Internet, go to a search engine site such as AltaVista (www.altavista.com) and research the following information to include in your brochure:

- The name, address, and phone number of the bed and breakfast in your chosen city.
- The price per night for a single and double room, using the local currency.
- A description of the hotel with a picture.
- Photos or pictures of the city or country in which your Inn is located.
- 3 short articles about your hotel and the interesting tourist attractions that are nearby, written by you, based on your research. You should write these articles using Microsoft Word, then save them with the filenames specified in the table below.

story title	story description	word count	save as file
Welcome to <City>	Describe the city, providing brief overview of key facts	100	City.doc
About the Inn	Describe the inn, it's offerings and amenities	100	Inn.doc.
What to do in <City>	Describe the key tourist attractions in your chosen city	100	Attractions.doc.

b. Open a new publication and choose the Borders Informational brochure from the New Publications task pane.

c. Type the name of your Bed and Breakfast in the top text box on the third panel of page 1. [If your name or another name appears as the Business Name in this panel, replace that with the name of your Bed and Breakfast.]

d. Replace the text in the Product/Services Information with a short phrase that summarizes the experience you want your guests to have (such as **A home away from home**).

e. Replace the placeholder photo in the third column of page 1 with a picture of an inn.

f. In the bottom text box in the third column of page 1, replace the placeholder phone number with the Inn's phone number. Insert the Inn's address in the text box above the phone number.

g. On page 2, Replace the "Main Inside Heading" placeholder text with the heading **Welcome to < your city>**, then replace the story placeholder text with the file City.doc that you created.

h. Replace the first Secondary Heading in column 2 of page 2 with the text **About Our Inn**, then replace the placeholder story text with your file Inn.doc.

i. Replace the second Secondary Heading with the title **What to do in <your city>**, then replace the placeholder story text under the heading with your file Attractions.doc.

j. On page 1, replace the placeholder text for the Back Panel Heading with **Why Not Book Now?**, then replace the story placeholder text with the file PB B-6.doc. Insert the rate information for your inn into the story.

k. Replace all the placeholder photos with images relating to your city or inn.

l. On the Second column of page 1, delete the placeholder logo, if necessary, then insert the name, address, and phone number of the inn in the empty text box at the bottom of the page.

m. Save your publication as Inn Brochure.pub, then spell check, print and close the publication.

▶ Visual Workshop

Create the advertisement for the play shown in Figure B-29. Use the Floating Oval Event Flyer Wizard. Replace the placeholder clip art with the image of Romeo and Juliet, which is available in the Clip Art task pane. Group the four text boxes containing date, time, location, and contact information, and then move them into the position shown. Insert your name in the Contact text box. In the black rectangle at the bottom of the page, insert a text box with two columns and insert the text file PB B-7.doc. (Hint: click inside the text box, press [Ctrl][A] to select all the text, then change the font color to white.) Insert a pull quote, choosing the Frames pull quote design from the Design Gallery. To create the WordArt shown, choose the Wave 1 shape. Save your publication with the name Play flyer.pub.

FIGURE B-29

Publisher 2002

Unit C

Creating
a Web Publication

Objectives

▶ **Understand and plan Web publications**
▶ **Create a new Web publication**
▶ **Format a Web publication**
▶ **Modify a Web form**
▶ **Add form controls**
▶ **Preview a Web publication**
▶ **Convert a Web publication to a Web site**
▶ **Convert a print publication to a Web site**

Publisher 2002 lets you quickly and easily create Web pages. You can start with a premade design and customize it to your needs. Publisher provides many tools that facilitate the development of Web pages. You can also convert an existing publication to a layout suitable for the Web. Karen Rosen produces a quarterly newsletter called *LoftLife* for MediaLoft employees. She will use one of the Web site designs available from the New Publication task pane to create a two-page *LoftLife* Web site for the company intranet. She will also convert the most recent issue to a Web layout.

Understanding and Planning Web Publications

The **World Wide Web**, or simply the **Web**, is a collection of electronic documents available to people around the world through the **Internet**, a global computer network. **Web pages** are the documents that make up the Web. A group of associated Web pages is known as a **Web site**. Anyone with Internet access can create Web pages and Web sites and add them to the network. **Web browsers** are the software that allow anyone to view Web sites. All Web pages are written in a common programming language called **Hypertext Markup Language (HTML)**. With Publisher, you can create a **Web publication**—a publication that you later convert to either a Web page or a Web site—without needing to know HTML. You can use the Publisher skills you already possess to design and create the content, and then let Publisher create the HTML code for you. Figure C-1 shows how a Web page created with Publisher looks in a browser. Karen plans which features she will add to her Web site. Figure C-2 shows a sketch of her plan.

Details

▶ A **hyperlink**, or simply a **link**, is specially formatted text or a graphic that a user can click to open an associated Web page. Links serve as the foundation of the Web. Almost all pages on the Web are connected to each other through a series of links because each Web page can contain many links to different Web sites. Karen will place a welcome paragraph on the home page that describes the features of *LoftLife Online*, and Karen will add a link to the Feedback Form on page 2.

▶ Much like their paper counterparts, a **Web form** can include areas for text input, such as name and address, and provide an easy way for a user to submit information. Unlike their paper counterparts, Web forms also can offer boxes that users click to submit information via the Web. Many organizations that do business online allow users to select products or services using a Web form. Karen will add a Feedback Form to *LoftLife Online*, where users can answer the Question of the Month and provide comments on the latest issue.

▶ When your Web site has multiple pages, it's important to provide users with an easy and consistent method of navigating between them. A **navigation bar** provides a set of links to the most important pages in a Web site, displayed in the same location on each page. When you create a Web publication using the New Publication task pane, Publisher can automatically create one or more navigation bars on the main pages and update them as you add or delete pages. Karen will have navigation bars at the top and bottom of both pages, making it easier for viewers to jump quickly to where they want to go.

FIGURE C-1: Web page created using Publisher

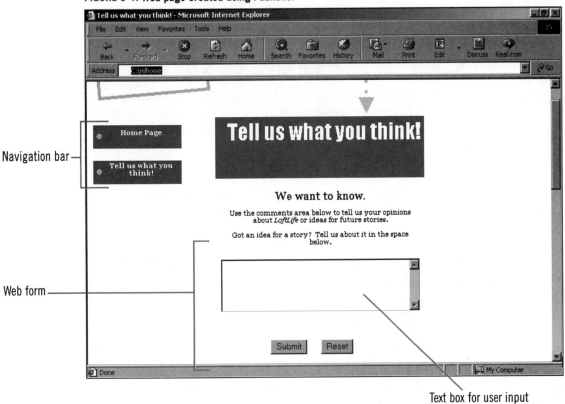

Navigation bar —

Web form —

Text box for user input

FIGURE C-2: Karen's sketch of the *LoftLife Online* Web site

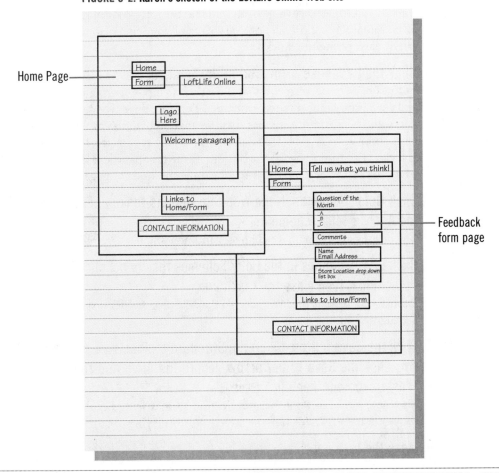

Home Page —

Feedback form page

Unit C

Publisher 2002

Creating a New Web Publication

You can use one of the Web site designs on the New Publication task pane to create a single Web page, or a Web site containing several pages. In either case, the first page you create is known as the **home page**. A home page is the introductory page of a Web site, which usually gives an overview of the site's contents and provides easy access to other pages in the Web site. If you want to create a Web presence but have little information to publicize, you may be able to fit all the information on a single Web page, which stands alone as your home page. 🔨 The MediaLoft Web site will eventually have many pages to include links to past issues of *LoftLife*. For now, though, Karen creates two pages—the home page and a feedback form using the New Publication task pane.

Steps

1. **Start Publisher, if the new Publication task page is not open, click File on the menu bar, then click New**
   The New Publication task pane opens.

2. **Click Web Sites in the By Publication Type list**
   The Publication Gallery displays sample home page layouts, as shown in Figure C-3.

> **Trouble?**
> If a dialog box asks you to enter information about yourself in the wizard, click OK, then click Cancel.

3. **Scroll down the Publication Gallery, then click the Mobile Web Site design**
   The Publication Gallery closes, and a new publication opens in the workspace with the Mobile Web site design. The Web Site Options task pane displays options for adding a navigation bar and a form. The navigation bar will contain links to all the pages in the Web site.

4. **Verify that the Multiple icon is selected in the Navigation bar section of the task pane**
   Clicking multiple places a navigation bar at the top (Vertical navigation bar) and the bottom (Horizontal navigation bar) of every page of your site, making it easy for users to view different parts of the site quickly.

5. **Click the Response form icon in the Form section of the task pane**
   Forms are Web page elements that allow users to input information, such as their name, address, and credit card number to place an order. There are three types of forms shown in the task pane. You want to include a response form so that MediaLoft employees can easily provide feedback about *LoftLife*. The Web site will have only two pages. If you want to add more pages you can click Insert page at the bottom of the task pane and add up to six different kinds of pages to the site. See Table C-1 for the different kinds of pages Publisher allows you to add.

6. **Click Color Schemes in the Web Site Options task pane, then click Wildflower from the Apply a color scheme list**
   The home page colors have changed, and now the bars are red.

7. **Click Font Schemes in the Color Schemes task pane, click Impact in the Apply a font scheme list, then close the task pane**
   Publisher reformats the Web page so that the placeholder text fonts are Impact and Georgia. See Figure C-4.

> **Trouble?**
> If a dialog box opens asking if you want to save the modified logo, click No.

8. **Click the Save button 🖫 on the Standard toolbar, type loftweb in the file name text box, click the Save in list arrow, locate the drive and the folder where your Project Files are stored, then click Save**
   The file is saved in Publisher publication format with a .pub file extension; later, you will convert it to HTML format, the format for displaying documents on the Web.

9. **Close the task pane**

FIGURE C-3: Web site designs in Publication Gallery

Web Sites category selected

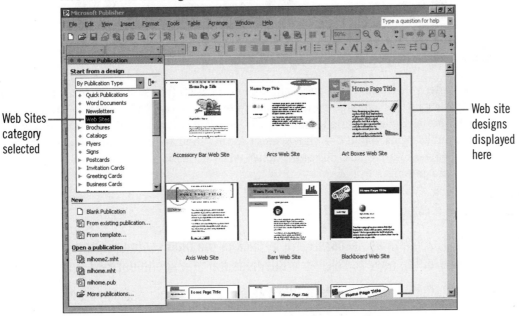

Web site designs displayed here

FIGURE C-4: New home page with Wildflower color scheme and Impact font scheme

Vertical navigation bar

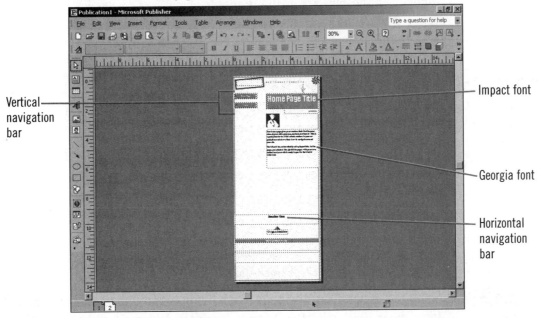

Impact font

Georgia font

Horizontal navigation bar

TABLE C-1: Types of Web pages you can create using the insert pages command from the task pane

web page type	useful for
Story	Organization's history, report of recent event, open letter
Calendar	List of upcoming important dates/events
Event	Information about an upcoming event
Special offer	Details of a sale or discount
Price list	Costs and descriptions of available products or services
Related links	Descriptions and links for other relevant Web sites

Publisher 2002

Formatting a Web Publication

After you create a Web publication using a design from the task pane, you need to personalize the contents and adjust the formatting to your needs. In addition to the standard formatting options available for all publications, Publisher offers several tools specifically for use in Web publications. Table C-2 shows these special toolbar buttons and explains how to use them. Karen starts customizing her Web publication by changing the default home page text and graphics.

Steps

Trouble?

The placeholder text may differ if the Personal Information dialog box has been completed for your installation of Publisher.

1. Zoom in as necessary, triple-click in the **blue rectangle frame** in the top-left corner of the page to select the **Business Name placeholder text**, then type **MediaLoft**

2. Click in the **Home Page Title frame** to select the placeholder text, then type **LoftLife Online**

3. Select the text **Your business tag line here.** in the frame below LoftLife Online, then type **What's up in the 'Loft?**

4. Right-click the **clip art** of the graduate, point to **Change Picture**, click **From File**, select **PB C-1.jpg** from the drive and folder where your Project Files are stored, then click **Insert**
   The MediaLoft logo now appears in the picture frame.

Trouble?

If a dialog box opens asking if you want to install the file converter, click Yes, then follow the onscreen instructions.

5. Right-click the first paragraph of text, point to **Change Text**, click **Text File**, select the **PB C-2.doc** from the drive and folder where your Project Files are stored, then click **OK**
   The new text now appears in the text box. Compare your screen with Figure C-5.

6. Select the text **Feedback Form** in the second paragraph you inserted, then click the **Insert Hyperlink button** on the Standard toolbar
   The Insert Hyperlink dialog box opens.

7. Click the **Place in This Document icon**, click **Page 2. Form** in the Select a place in this document list, then click **OK**
   The text "Feedback Form" now appears underlined and in color, indicating that it is now a link that viewers can click to open the page that contains the feedback form.

Trouble?

If the text boxes differ, it's because your personal information has been set up. Use Figure C-6 as a guide to delete one text box, add text and resize the text box below the red box.

8. Scroll to the bottom of the page, click the **pyramid image** to select the **Organization logo**, press **[Del]**, click the **Primary Business Address text box frame** at the bottom of the page, press **[Del]**, click the text box with phone numbers below **To Contact Us:**, drag the lower-middle sizing handle to the 13-inch mark on the vertical ruler, then type the contact information and format the text for MediaLoft as shown in Figure C-6

9. Save the publication

FIGURE C-5: Top section of home page completed

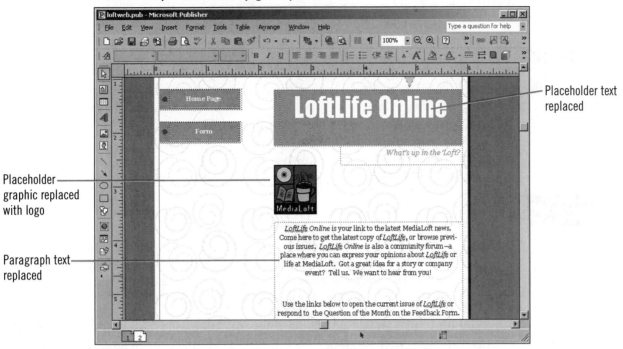

Placeholder text replaced

Placeholder graphic replaced with logo

Paragraph text replaced

FIGURE C-6: *LoftLife* contact information

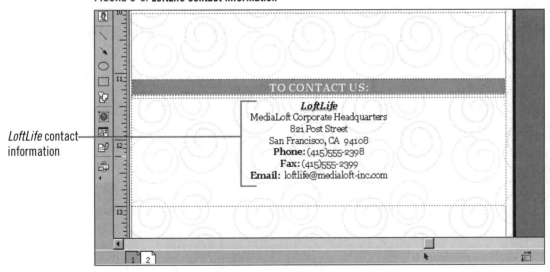

LoftLife contact information

TABLE C-2: Web Page Formatting Options

option	button	description
Hot Spot Tool		Formats a single graphic with links to multiple Web pages
Form Control		Inserts a form field for user input, such as a text box or check box
HTML Code Fragment		Allows advanced users to add additional HTML code to a specific part of a publication
Insert Hyperlink		Adds a hyperlink to the selected object
Web Page Preview		Opens the current Web page using your system's default Web browser

Modifying a Web Form

Including a form in a Web page is a great way to encourage users to interact with your organization. With forms you can collect valuable information, such as customer names and addresses, or feedback on a product. The response form that Karen selected in the Web Options task pane contains four placeholder questions, a comments text area, and user contact information text boxes. ✏️ Karen wants to customize the response form provided through the task pane by changing the form headings and modifying one of the questions. She deletes the other three questions and rearranges the remaining objects.

Steps

1. **Click the Page 2 navigation button** then zoom in on the top of the page
   The publication's second page contains the feedback form you selected in the Web Page Options task pane. Notice that several of the text fields reflect formatting changes that you made to corresponding fields on the home page.

2. Click **Form Page Title**, type **Tell us what you think!**, click **General Response Form Title**, type **We want to know.**, click **Briefly describe your desired feedback**, then type **Answer the question below and use the comments area to tell us your opinions about *LoftLife*.**
   Compare your screen with Figure C-7.

3. Click **First Question**, type **Which job perk is most important to you?**, click **Answer A**, type **Flextime**, click **Answer B**, type **Free beverages**, click **Answer C**, then type **Telecommuting policy**
   The question and three choices are complete. You can select multiple objects by dragging the mouse diagonally to create a rectangular shape around the objects. This is called dragging a selection rectangle.

   Trouble?
   Be sure to include all parts of each object when dragging a selection rectangle. If your selection box doesn't include all the desired objects or you select too many objects, press [Esc] and try again.

4. Drag a selection rectangle around the **Third Question and its three answers** and the **Fourth Question and its three answers** to select all eight objects, then press **[Delete]**
   You deleted two of the placeholder questions and answer options.

5. Drag a selection rectangle around the **Second Question and its three answers**, then press **[Delete]**
   One question remains on the form.

6. Drag a selection rectangle around the **Comments label** and the **Comments multiline text box** to select both objects, then drag them up until they are just below Telecommuting policy
   Compare your screen with Figure C-8.

7. Save your changes

FIGURE C-7: **Form Page with new heading text**

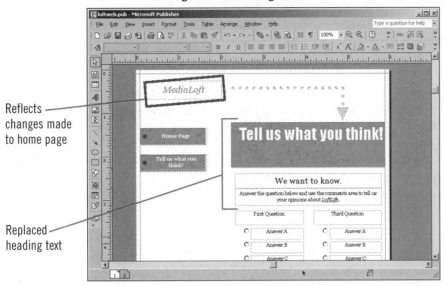

Reflects
changes made
to home page

Replaced
heading text

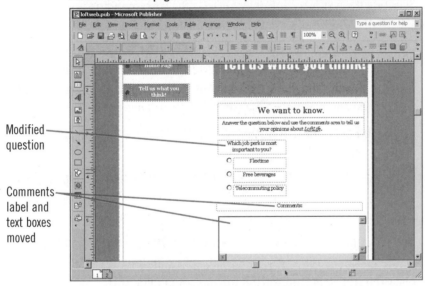

Modified
question

Comments
label and
text boxes
moved

Adding multimedia components to a Web publication

In addition to including text and graphics in your Web sites, Publisher allows you to add multimedia elements to make the site more eye-catching and to make more information available to your viewers. The Web Site Options task pane lets you select a background fill, as well as sound, for your site, which plays on the user's browser when the page opens. To insert and format a sound, click Background Fill and sound on the Web Site Options task pane, click Background sound to open the Web Options dialog box, then type a sound file location in the Background sound file name text box. You can choose to have the sound loop continuously or play as many times as you specify.

You can add simple animation to a site by inserting an animated GIF. GIF is a standard format for dis-

playing images on Web pages. An animated GIF is a short animation encoded in the same format, which plays repeatedly when it opens in a browser. The Web site you converted the newsletter to contained an animated wheel at the top of the home page. To add GIFs to your Web publication, click Insert on the menu bar, point to Picture, click From File, then type the name and location of the .gif file you want to add. Some .gif files are available in the Clip Organizer.

You can also add video and other objects by selecting Object on the Insert menu, clicking the Create from File option button, then specifying the object's location in the dialog box.

Adding Form Controls

Each item in a form, such as a text box or a check box, is known as a **form control**. HTML allows Web pages to use seven different types of form controls to collect information from users, as shown in Table C-3. Each control is usually associated with a text box, which can display a label or question, or provide guidance to the user about the type of information to be collected. Karen customizes the Feedback Form further by modifying the contact information form controls and labels. She deletes some of the default controls and labels to make it less cluttered, and leaves the controls and labels for a name and an e-mail address. She also adds a drop-down list for users to provide their store location.

Steps

1. Scroll down as necessary, click the **Address:** label for the first single-line text box, then type **Name:**

2. Click the **City single-line text box control**, then press **[Del]**
   Selecting the text box control also selects the corresponding text box label because the two objects are grouped.

3. Delete the text box controls and corresponding text labels for **State/Prov.**, **Country**, **Zip/Post. Code**, and **Phone**, then drag the **Name** and **E-mail controls and label**, the **Submit button**, and the **Reset button** to the positions shown in Figure C-9
   You deleted and rearranged the controls to better meet your needs.

4. Click the **Form Control button** 📧 on the Objects toolbar, then click **List Box**
   A list box appears showing three items.

5. Drag the **lower middle resizing handle** of the list box up so that only Item One appears, then drag the **list box** to just below the E-mail: text box control
   You modified the list box to show only one item at a time.

6. Double-click the **list box**, make sure **Item One** is selected in the Appearance section of the List Box Properties dialog box, click **Modify**, type **Boston** in the Item text box, click the **Not Selected option button**, then click **OK**

7. Click **Item Two**, click **Modify**, type **Chicago**, click **OK**, click **Item Three**, click **Modify**, type **Houston**, then click **OK**
   The List Box Properties dialog box shows three items: Boston, Chicago, and Houston.

8. Click **Add**, type **Kansas City** in the Item text box, click **OK**, click **Add**, type **New York**, click **OK**, click **Add**, type **San Diego**, click **OK**, click **Add**, type **San Francisco**, click **OK**, click **Add**, type **Seattle**, click **OK**, then click **OK**
   The list box displays the text "Boston." MediaLoft employees who use this form will be able to click the arrow next to the text and select the city where they work.

QuickTip

Click the label, press and hold [Shift], click the text box control then click the Group objects button 🔲 then move them together as a group.

9. Click the **Text Box button** 📧 on the Objects toolbar, drag to create a text box to the left of the list box you just created that is the same size as the E-mail label above, then type **Store:**
   The list box now has a Store label next to it. Compare your screen with Figure C-10.

10. Double-click the **Submit button**, click **Form Properties**, click the **Save the data in a file on my Web server option button**, click **OK** twice, then save your publication
    All data entered by users will be stored in a file on the MediaLoft Web server.

FIGURE C-9: Form page with deleted and moved controls and labels

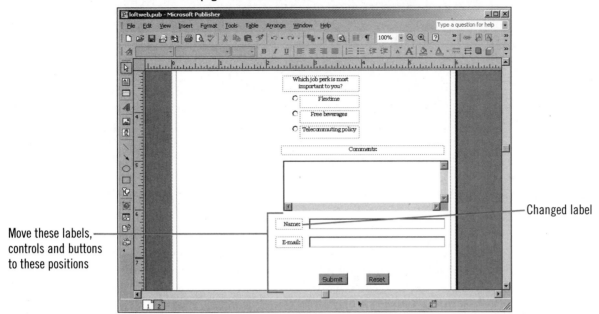

Changed label

Move these labels,
controls and buttons
to these positions

FIGURE C-10: Completed form

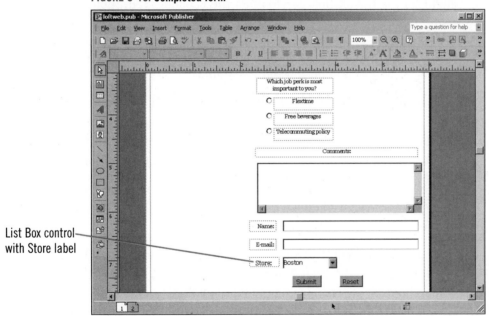

List Box control
with Store label

TABLE C-3: Web Page Form Controls

control name	uses
Single-line Text Box	Short input, such as a name or e-mail address
Multi-line Text Box	Longer input, such as comments
Check Box	A question or option that the user can select, such as not being added to a mailing list
Option Button	A list of choices, of which the user should pick a limited number
List Box	A drop-down menu providing a list of choices
Submit Button	A command button, used to submit information entered in the form
Reset Button	A command button, used to clear information from a form

Previewing a Web Publication

Creating and editing your Web publication in Publisher gives you an idea of the appearance of your final Web site. However, whenever you develop a Web site, it's best to look at the publication in a Web browser before actually turning it into a Web site and making it available on a network. Because some aspects of the publication can appear differently in a browser, Publisher provides a tool that lets you preview the publication in a Web browser to ensure that it appears the way you want. Upon review, you can make changes to the publication, if necessary, before publishing it on a network. ✐ Karen previews *LoftLife Online* in her browser and makes final adjustments.

Steps

1. Click the **Web Page Preview button** 🖳 on the Standard toolbar, click the **Web site option button** (if it is not already selected), then click **OK**
   Publisher creates a temporary version of your Web site in HTML and opens the file in your Web browser, as shown in Figure C-11.

2. Scroll down the home page to view the entire contents, click **Tell us what you think!** on the navigation bar to open the second page, then scroll to view all the contents of page 2
   You notice that you need to delete the placeholder logo on page 2 and adjust the size of some of the text boxes containing the information on page 2. Both pages contain large gaps between the elements at the top and the bottom.

3. Click the **loftweb.pub-Microsoft Publisher program button** on the taskbar, click the **page 2 Navigation button**, drag the right-middle sizing handle on the question text box to the right so that the question fits on one line, delete the **placeholder logo**, then resize the contact information text box so that all the information is visible

4. Click the **page 1 Navigation button** of the publication, click the **Zoom list arrow** on the Standard toolbar, then click **Whole Page**
   You can now view the whole page.

5. Drag a selection rectangle to select all the objects at the bottom of the page, as shown in Figure C-12, then drag the selected items up so that the top of the selected section lines up at the 7-inch mark on the vertical ruler
   The entire contents of the home page are now closer to the top of the page.

6. Click the **page 2 Navigation button**, drag a selection rectangle to select all the objects at the bottom of the page, then drag the selected items up to that they begin approximately at the 8-inch mark on the vertical ruler

7. Save your publication, click **NO** if asked to save the modified logo, click the **Web Page Preview button** 🖳, click the **Web Site option button**, then click **OK**
   The home page appears with all the elements consolidated, as shown in Figure C-13.

8. Test the links on the navigation bar to view the second page, then click the link to return to the home page

FIGURE C-11: Preview of home page in browser

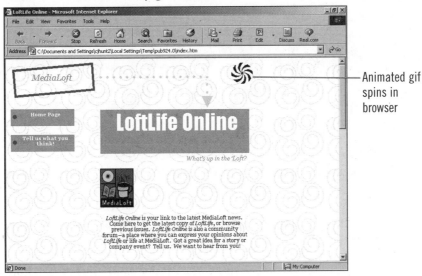

Animated gif spins in browser

FIGURE C-12: Selected objects at the bottom of the home page

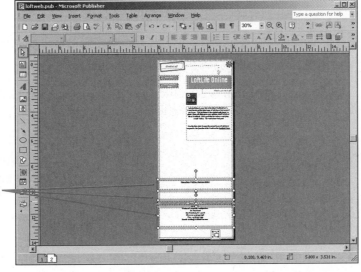

Objects selected using selection rectangle

FIGURE C-13: Preview of home page with lower objects moved up

Lower objects now closer to top of page

Converting a Web Publication to a Web Site

In your work on the Web site so far, you have edited and saved the publication in the Publisher file format (which has the file extension .pub). When you are satisfied with the publication's appearance and layout, you need to convert the publication to HTML format (which has the file extension .htm). The HTML document you produce can then be published on a network (either the Internet or an intranet) and displayed by Web browsers. ✎ Karen is satisfied with the preview of her Web site in the Web browser and is ready to convert the publication to an HTML document.

1. If necessary, click the **loftweb.pub Microsoft Publisher program button** on the taskbar to open the Publisher window containing *LoftLife Online*

2. Click **File** on the menu bar, then click **Save As Web Page**
   The Save as dialog box opens, as shown in Figure C-14.

Trouble?

Be sure to select the drive and folder where your Project Files are stored.

3. Click the **Create New Folder button** 🗂, type **loft_on** in the Name text box, click **OK**, then click **Save**
   This creates a separate folder just for this Web site so that all the files, including the graphics for the top and bottom page borders, are grouped together. The Save as Web Page dialog box displays a status indicator as Publisher saves the publication in HTML format.

4. Click **File** on the menu bar, click **Close**, start Internet Explorer (or your default browser), click **File** on the Internet Explorer menu bar, click **Open**, click **Browse**, open the **loft_on folder** where you saved the .HTML file, click **loftweb.htm**, click **Open**, then click **OK**
   The *LoftLine Online* Web page, now saved as an HTML file, appears in your default Web browser.

5. Click the **Tell us what you think! link** on the navigation bar
   The second page of the Web site opens, as shown in Figure C-15.

6. Type *your name* in the Name text box control, click **File** on the menu bar, click **Print**, click **Print**, click the **Home Page link** on the navigation bar, click **File** on the menu bar, click **Print**, then click **Print**
   You printed both the home page and the form page of your Web site.

7. Click **File** on the Internet Explorer menu bar, then click **Close**
   You exited the browser but Publisher is still running.

FIGURE C-14: **Save As dialog box**

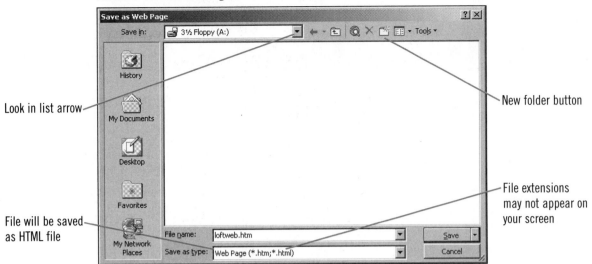

Look in list arrow

New folder button

File extensions may not appear on your screen

File will be saved as HTML file

FIGURE C-15: **Feedback form page in Web browser**

CLUES TO USE

Formatting Web publications for different audiences

When you create a Web page, you want to make it available to the largest possible audience. Publisher allows you to create Web pages for Internet Explorer 4.0 or later, or Netscape Navigator 4.0 or later. If your site is going to be viewed on a corporate intranet, where all users have Internet Explorer 5.5, you might want to optimize your site and include features that can only be viewed with this version of the browser. However, if your site is being viewed on the Internet by a wide range of users, you will want to make sure that you optimize the site for an earlier browser version. To optimize your site for a specific browser click Tools on the menu bar, click Options, then click Web Options. Click the browsers tab, click the browser for which you want to optimize your site in the Target Browsers list, then click OK.

Converting a Print Publication to a Web Site

When you create a Web site from scratch, you format the text, preview it using the Web Page Preview button, make adjustments as necessary, and then save it as a Web page. You can use this same process to convert print publications such as flyers and newsletters into Web pages. Karen wants to start making the *LoftLife* newsletter available on the MediaLoft intranet. She starts by converting a recent issue to a Web publication.

1. **Click File on the menu bar, click Open, open the file PB C-3.pub from the drive and folder where your Project Files are stored**
   The first page of *LoftLife* appears in the workspace.

2. **Click View on the menu bar, then click Task Pane to open the Newsletter Options task pane if it is not already open**
   The Newsletter Options task pane opens.

3. **Click Convert to Web Layout at the bottom of the Newsletter Options task pane**
   The newsletter appears in Web format in the workspace as a 10-page publication, and the Web Site Options task pane displays options for formatting the Web site. See Figure C-16.

4. **Close the task pane, then use the Zoom feature and the page navigation buttons to explore the Web publication pages**
   In order to lay out existing publications as Web sites, you must decide the order of the stories and the relation of the elements in a publication. Because the newsletter is a long and fairly complex publication, Publisher automatically puts each story on its own page, regardless of how much room it needs. You need to adjust the Web site's layout so that it makes sense. Notice that each page containing a story includes placeholder pull quotes and graphics. Notice, too, that the pages need a lot of adjusting. Text boxes are spilling off the page and overlapping with each other. You need to spend considerable time finalizing the layout using Publisher skills. You can also add hyperlinks to lead users from page to page throughout a story. However, using the Convert to Web layout feature gives you a good head start in getting the project done.

5. **Click File on the menu bar, click Close, then click No**
   Karen realizes she has a lot of work to do to convert the newsletter to a Web site. She plans on sketching out a plan for how the site will be structured. When her plan is complete, she will go back and use her Publisher skills to format the pages and link them so that viewers can find the information they need.

6. **Exit Publisher**

FIGURE C-16: *LoftLife* issue converted to Web publication

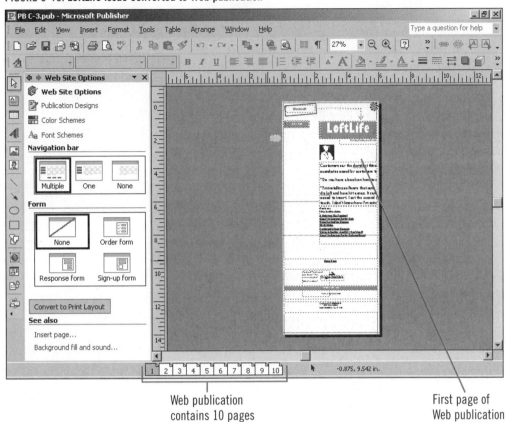

Web publication
contains 10 pages

First page of
Web publication

Publishing a Web site

If you want to make your Web site available to all users of the Internet, you need to publish it, or store your Web site files on a Web server known as a host. A Web server is always connected to the Web, making your pages available to anyone with Web access. If you already have an account with a commercial Internet Service Provider (ISP) or a school, room for your Web site on the Web server may be included with the account. Additionally, several Internet companies offer free space for Web pages on their servers; in exchange, they place an advertisement on each page in your Web site. All Web servers impose limits on the amount of data you can store; be sure to check these limits before publishing your Web site. A graphics-heavy site can quickly mushroom in size, so it is important to place graphics sparingly in your Web if your allotted space is small. There are many ways to publish your Web site. If you are using Microsoft Windows ME or Windows 98, you can use the Microsoft Web Publishing Wizard. To start the Wizard, click Start on the Start menu, click Programs, click Accessories, click Internet Tools, then click Web Publishing Wizard. Answer the questions posed to you by the Wizard to publish your site to the Web.

Publisher 2002

Practice

▶ Concepts Review

Label each item marked in Figure C-17.

FIGURE C-17

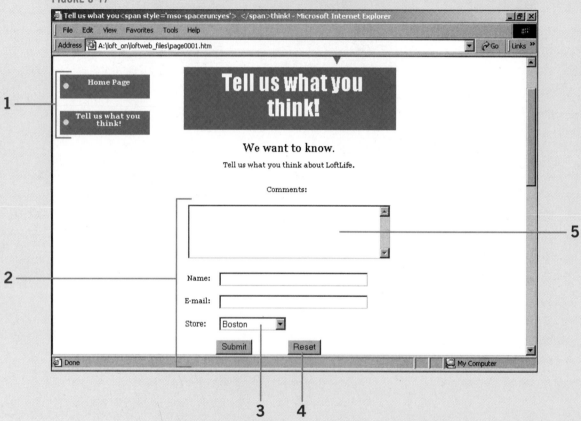

Match each item with its definition.

6. **HTML**
7. **Web form**
8. **browser**
9. **home page**
10. **navigation bar**
11. **Web site**

a. A means for users of a Web page to enter and submit information
b. The introductory page of a Web site
c. Special software for viewing Web pages and Web sites
d. The programming language in which all Web pages are created
e. Area on a Web page that provides links to the most important pages in a Web site, in the same location on each page
f. A group of associated Web pages

Select the best answer from the list of choices.

12. **Which Web page control would most commonly be found in a form?**
    a. Image box
    b. Link
    c. Navigation bar
    d. Check box
13. **Which is not true about Web pages and Web sites?**
    a. They can be created and added to the network by anyone with Internet access.
    b. They can be created only by using software designed exclusively for that purpose.
    c. They can be viewed with special software called Web browsers.
    d. They are written in a common programming language called Hypertext Markup Language (HTML).
14. **If you want a user to open a Web page by clicking on text or graphics, you insert a(n):**
    a. Hyperlink.
    b. User input field.
    c. Form control.
    d. HTML code fragment.
15. **You can create a Web publication from a print publication by:**
    a. Using the Save As Web Page command.
    b. Selecting the Page Setup command.
    c. Using the Web Publishing Wizard.
    d. Using the Convert to Web layout command.

▶ Skills Review

1. **Create a new Web publication.**
   a. Start Publisher, then, if necessary, open the New Publication task pane.
   b. In the By Publication Type list in the task pane, click Web Sites, then click the Spotlight Web Site design in the Publication Gallery.
   c. In the Web Site Options task pane, verify that Multiple is selected in the Navigation bar area.
   d. In the Form section, click Sign-up form.
   e. Choose the Prairie Color Scheme.
   f. Choose the Facet Font Scheme, then close the task pane.
2. **Format a Web publication.**
   a. Zoom in on the top of the Web page, click the image of the pagoda at the top of the page, right-click, point to Change Picture, click From File, select the file PB C-4.jpg from the drive and folder where your Project Files are located, then click Insert.
   b. Replace the graphic of a dragon with a clip art image of your choice relating to sports, and size it appropriately.
   c. Select the text Home Page Title, then type **MediaLoft Recreation**.
   d. Select the text Your business tag line here placeholder text below MediaLoft Recreation, then type **And you thought your job was fun!**
   e. Delete the pyramid placeholder logo and graphic at the bottom of the page.
   f. Right-click the paragraph placeholder text, point to Change Text, click Text File, then insert the file PB C-5.doc from the drive and folder where your Project Files are located. Click No in the Autoflow alert window, then drag the bottom of the text frame down until all text is visible and the Text in Overflow icon disappears.
   g. Select the text "sign-up form" in the last line of the paragraph before Boston, then click the Insert Hyperlink button on the Standard toolbar.

h. Click the Place in This Document option, click Page 2, Form, then click OK.

i. Scroll to the bottom of the page, then type the following information in the two adjacent text boxes below:

To contact us:

MediaLoft, Inc. Your name 821 Post Street San Francisco, CA 94108	Phone: 415-555-2398 Fax: 415-555-2399 Email: Recreation@medialoft-inc.com

j. Resize the text box as necessary to make the text fit, then save your publication as **recsite** to the drive and folder where your Project Files are stored. Do not save the logo.

3. Modify a Web form.

a. Open page 2 of the publication and zoom in on the top of the page.

b. Select the text Form Page Title, then type **Event Registration**.

c. Replace Sign-up Form Title with **Sign up today for your store's event!**

d. Drag a selection rectangle to select all the controls and text labels from the Sign up for: label through the Total: control, then press [Delete].

e. Select and delete the text labels and controls for Country, Zip/Post. code, and Phone, delete all the labels and controls from Method of Payment through Exp. Date, then scroll down and delete the pyramid place-holder graphic.

f. Replace the text in the label "Address" with **Event**, then replace the label text "State/Prov." with **Number of Guests**.

g. Drag the E-mail: control and label up until it is just below the City: control and label.

h. Drag the Submit and Reset buttons up so they are positioned just below the E-mail control.

4. Add form controls.

a. Click the City: label and text box, click the Ungroup Objects button, select only the City text box, then press [Delete].

b. Click the Form Control button, click List Box, drag to create a one-line list box in the space formerly occupied by the City text box, then double-click the list box you inserted.

c. Make sure Item One is selected in the Appearance section, click Modify, replace the text in the Item text box with **Boston**, click the Not Selected option button, then click OK.

d. Replace the Item text with **Chicago** for Item Two, and with **Houston** for Item Three.

e. Click Add, type **Kansas City** in the Item text box, click OK, create four new items with the text **New York**, **San Diego**, **San Francisco**, and **Seattle**, then click OK to close the List Box Properties dialog box.

f. Double-click the Submit button, click Form Properties, click the Save the data in a file on my Web server option button, click OK, click OK, then save your changes.

5. Preview a Web publication.

a. Click the Web Page Preview button, verify that the Web site option button is selected.

b. Scroll down your home page to view the entire contents, click Event Registration on the navigation bar to open the second page, then scroll to view all the page's contents.

c. Click the Publisher Program Button on the taskbar, go to page 2.

d. Drag a selection rectangle to select all objects from the Name label to the Reset button, then drag them up to just below "Sign up today for your store's event!"

e. Click the Page 1 navigation button, drag to select the MediaLoft Address at the bottom of the page, click the Copy button on the Standard toolbar, click the Page 2 navigation button, select the contact information in the text box at the bottom of the page, click the Paste Button on the Standard toolbar, then drag the lower middle sizing handle of the text box down so that all the contact information is visible.

f. Drag a selection rectangle to select the Home Page and Event Registration links and the contact information text boxes, then drag them up to just below the Submit and Reset buttons.

g. Save your changes, click the Web Page Preview button, verify that the Web site option button is selected, click OK, and review your changes.

h. Close the browser window.

6. **Convert a Web publication to a Web site.**

a. Click the Publisher program button on the taskbar if it is not open to view the recsite publication.

b. Click File on the menu bar, then click Save As Web Page.

c. Locate the drive and folder where your Project Files are stored, click the Create New Folder button, type **mediarec** as the new folder name, click OK, then click Save.

d. Open your default Web browser. Click File on the menu bar, click Open, open the mediarec folder, double-click the file recsite.htm, then click OK.

e. Click the Event Registration button on the navigation bar.

f. Type your name in the Name field, click the Print button on the browser toolbar. Click the home Page link, then print that page.

g. Close the Browser window.

h. Close the recsite.htm file, but keep Publisher open.

7. **Convert a print publication to a Web site.**

a. Open the file PB C-6.pub from the drive and folder where your Project Files are stored.

b. In the Brochure Options task pane, click Convert to Web layout.

c. In the Web options task pane, verify that the Multiple icon in the navigation bar section is selected, then click None in the Form section.

d. Starting on page 1, use your Publisher skills to arrange the text and graphics on the pages appropriately, resizing, moving and arranging text and graphics as necessary. Replace placeholder graphics with appropriate pieces of clip art.

e. In an appropriate place on the home page, type **Designed by** *Your Name*, then save the file as a Web page with the name **fund.htm** in a folder called **fund** to the drive and folder where your Project Files are stored.

f. Open the pages in your browser, test the links, then print the pages from the browser.

g. Close your browser, then exit Publisher, do not save the publication.

► Independent Challenge 1

You have been hired by a local café to advertise their Saturday Karaoke Night series. You have decided to create a Web page describing the series that the café can publish on their ISP's (Internet Service Provider's) Web server. You start by creating a Web publication.

a. Start Publisher, then create a new Web publication using the Radial Web Site design.

b. Choose Multiple navigation bars, then insert a sign-up form on the second page.

c. Choose a Color Scheme and Font Scheme that appeals to you.

d. Replace the text Home Page Title with **Sing at Java Jerry's Café!**, delete the business tag line placeholder, replace the main paragraph text with the contents of the file PB C-7.doc, and do not use AutoFlow. Expand the text box so you can see all the text,

e. Delete the placeholder logo near the bottom of the page and replace the graphic with an appropriate piece of clip art.

f. Scroll to the bottom of the page, and insert the following text in the text box below To contact us:
Your Name, Karaoke Coordinator
Phone: 415-555-5232
E-mail: javajerryscafe@isp-services.com
98 Danvers Street
San Francisco, CA 94114

g. Save the publication with the name **karaoke**.

h. Open page 2 of the publication, replace the text Form Page Title with **Karaoke Night Registration**, replace the Sign-Up Form Title text with **Sing at Java Jerry's!**, delete all the labels and controls from Sign up for through Total, then delete all the labels and controls from Method of Payment through Exp. date: and the placeholder logo.

i. Just below the E-mail label, insert a text box for a label, then type **Song style** in it to create a song style label.

j. Insert a list box to the right of the Song style label that contains the following items **Country**, **R&B**, **Pop**, **Showtunes**, **Hip Hop**, and **Other**, resize the list box so that only the first item is showing.

k. Drag the remaining controls and labels up to fill in the empty space on the page, double-click the Submit button, click the Save the data in a file on my Web server option button, click OK, then save your publication.

l. Preview your page in a Web browser, then make any necessary formatting adjustments in Publisher, save your publication as a Web page named **karaoke.htm** in a folder called **karaoke** in the drive and folder where your Project Files are stored.

m. Print the pages, close your browser, close the publication, then exit Publisher.

 # Independent Challenge 2

You are the human resources director for Jasmine Herbal Harvest, a producer of herbal products. You are conducting a contest for your sales force, offering prizes for the best success story relating to your line of herbal products. You will post the information about the contest on your company intranet.

a. Start Publisher. Create a Web site using one of the Web site designs in the New Publication task pane.

b. Add multiple navigation bars and a response form.

c. Choose a color and font scheme that you like, and replace any graphics with appropriate ones.

d. Insert the following text on your home page, replacing the placeholder text as appropriate:
Jasmine Herbal Harvest, Inc., 2230 Red Rock Way, Sedona, Arizona 86336, (520) 555-9010

e. Type your name somewhere on the home page, and delete the placeholder logos on both pages.

f. On the home page, replace the paragraph text with the file PB C-8.doc. Don't use Autoflow and be sure you can view all the text in the text box.

g. Create a link from "Contest Form" at the end of the paragraph to the Contest form on page 2.

h. On page 2, replace the placeholder Form headings with the following:

Form Heading Placeholder	Replace with:
Form Page Title	Success Story Contest
General Response Form Title	Win a Caribbean Cruise for two!
Briefly describe your desired feedback	Describe the best success story you've heard from a customer about Jasmine Herbal Harvest products.

i. Delete all the placeholder questions, and the comments label, then drag the text box control up to close up the empty space.

j. Modify the remaining placeholder controls and labels so that the form contains only an E-mail label and text box and Submit and Reset buttons. Create a list box below the E-mail text box with four items as follows: **North**, **South**, **East**, **West**, then add a label with the text **Sales Territory**.

k. Drag all the remaining elements up to close up the space. Delete the placeholder logo.

l. Double-click the Submit button, click the save data in a file on my Web server option button, then click OK.

m. Preview your Publication in a browser using the Web Page Preview button, then make necessary changes. Save the publication as a Web page called **jasmine.htm**, in a new folder called **jasmine** in the drive and folder where your Project Files are stored.

n. View the pages in your browser, print both pages, close the browser, then exit Publisher.

► Independent Challenge 3

Create a Web site about yourself using your Publisher Web site creation skills.

a. Start by planning the information you want to include in your site. Remember that you can include several pages in your site, so you should plan on breaking the information up logically into separate Web pages. Make a list of information you want your site to contain, and create an outline of the site showing what information will appear on each page.

b. Start Publisher, choose a Web Site design from the New Publication task pane, then select the options you want to use for your Web site. In addition to your home page, include at least one Story page, and one Form page. You may include other pages if you want.

c. Replace the placeholder text and graphics on your Web site with graphics that are appropriate for you. If you need to add additional pages, click Insert page on the Web Site Options task pane. Publisher inserts a new page after the currently selected page.

d. Save your publication with the name **myweb.pub**.

e. Preview your Publication in a browser using the Web Page Preview button, make necessary changes, then use the Save As Web Page command to save the file as myweb.htm to a new folder called **mywebpg**.

f. View the pages in a browser, print the pages, close the browser, close the file, then exit Publisher. Do not save the modified logo.

Independent Challenge 4

There are many organizations that help people worldwide. Pick a cause that is important to you that works in the global community. It could be a health issue, a political cause, or a charitable organization. Create a Web site about this topic.

a. Log on to the Internet, go to a search engine site such as AltaVista, (www.altavista.com), and research your chosen topic. Be sure to find out how organizations work around the world to help and support this cause.

b. To create the Web site, choose a Web site design, color scheme, and font scheme that appeal to you, and appropriate graphics. Your site should have at least three pages, including a home page, a Response Form page, and a Related Links page. On the home page, include a paragraph written by you that provides an overview of the topic. Insert links from the paragraph to the Related Links page and the Response Form page.

c. On the Related Links page, insert at least five links to other Web sites that relate to your topic.

d. On the Response Form page, include at least one survey question for your viewers to answer relating to your cause.

e. Type your name somewhere on the Web page, use the Web page preview button to preview your work, then make any necessary adjustments in Publisher. Save your publication as **mycause.pub**, then save it as a Web page named **mycause.htm** in a folder called **my_cause**.

f. View the page in Publisher, view the page in your default browser. Print your pages.

g. Exit Publisher.

▶ Visual Workshop

Use Publisher to create the Web page shown in Figure C-18. Use the Bars Web design, the Trout color scheme, and the Industrial font scheme. Move the coffee cup graphic to the position shown in the figure, then import the paragraph text from the file PB C-9.doc. Format the paragraph text in Franklin Gothic Book 11 point. Resize the text box so that the paragraph fits as shown. Create the controls shown using the Web form control button. Add the E-mail label. Type your name in the E-mail text box on the page, save the publication as **inn_site.pub**, then save it as a Web page called **innsite.htm** in a new folder titled **inn**. View the publication in your default browser then print it. Close the browser, then exit Publisher.

FIGURE C-18

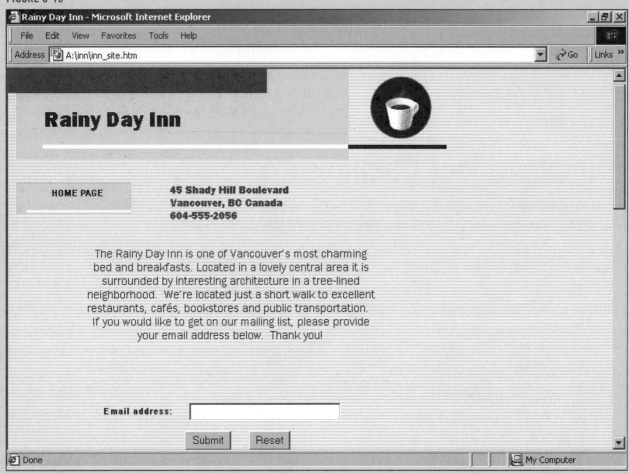

Project Files List

Read the following information carefully!

It is very important to organize and keep track of the files you need for this book.

1. **Find out from your instructor the location of the Project Files you need and the location where you will store your files.**

   - To complete many of the units in this book, you need to use Project Files. Your instructor will either provide you with a copy of the Project Files or ask you to make your own copy.

   - If you need to make a copy of the Project Files, you will need to copy a set of files from a file server, stand-alone computer, or the Web to the drive and folder where you will be storing your Project Files.

   - Your instructor will tell you which computer, drive letter, and folders contain the files you need, and where you will store your files.

   - You can also download the files by going to www.course.com. See the inside back cover of the book for instructions on how to download your files.

   ---

2. **Copy and organize your Project Files.**

   ### Floppy disk users

   - If you are using floppy disks to store your Project Files, the list on the following pages shows which files you'll need to copy onto your disk(s).

   - Unless noted in the Project Files List, you will need one formatted, high-density disk for each unit. For each unit you are assigned, copy the files listed in the **Project File Supplied column** onto one disk.

   - Make sure you label each disk clearly with the unit name (e.g., Publisher Unit A).

   - When working through the unit, save all your files to this disk.

   ### Users storing files in other locations

   - If you are using a zip drive, network folder, hard drive, or other storage device, use the Project Files List to organize your files.

   - Create a subfolder for each unit in the location where you are storing your files, and name it according to the unit title (e.g., Publisher Unit A).

   - For each unit you are assigned, copy the files listed in the **Project File Supplied column** into that unit's folder.

   - Store the files you modify or create for each unit in the unit folder.

   ---

3. **Find and keep track of your Project Files and completed files.**

   - Use the **Project File Supplied column** to make sure you have the files you need before starting the unit or exercise indicated in the **Unit and Location column**.

   - Use the **Student Saves File As column** to find out the filename you use when saving your changes to a Project File that was provided.

   - Use the **Student Creates File column** to find out the filename you use when saving a file you create new for the exercise.

Unit and Location	Project File Supplied	Student Saves File As	Student Creates File
Publisher Unit A			
Lessons	PB A-1.doc		Picnic.pub
	PB A-2.jpg		
Skills Review	PB A-3.doc		Apartment.pub
Independent Challenge 1	PB A-4.doc		Kittens.pub
Independent Challenge 2	PB A-5.doc		Washington.pub
Independent Challenge 3			Calendar.pub
Independent Challenge 4	PB A-6.doc		London.pub
Visual Workshop			Grand Opening.pub
Publisher Unit B*			

*Because the files created in this unit are large, you cannot open and then save the files with a new name to the same floppy disk. You will need to make backup copies of your Project Files before beginning this unit. The files created in this unit are large. If you are using floppy disks, you will need to organize the files for this unit onto 2 floppy disks. Copy the files as outlined above, and label each disk clearly (e.g., Publisher Unit B Disk 1).

Unit and Location	Project File Supplied	Student Saves File As	Student Creates File
Disk 1			
Lessons	Loftlife.pub	Loftlife.pub	
	PB B-1.doc		
Disk 2			
Skills Review	Rental.pub	Rental.pub	
	PB B-2.doc		
Independent Challenge 1	Nova Scotia.pub	Nova Scotia.pub	
	PB B-3.doc		
Independent Challenge 2	Fundraiser.pub	Fundraiser.pub	
	PB B-4.doc		
Independent Challenge 3	PB B-5.doc		Food Recovery.pub
Independent Challenge 4	PB B-6.doc		Inn Brochure.pub
			City.doc
			Inn.doc
			Attractions.doc
Visual Workshop	PB B-7.doc		Play flyer.pub
Publisher Unit C*			

*Because the files created in this unit are large, if you are using floppy disks, you will need to organize the files for this unit onto seven floppy disks if you are using floppies. Copy the files as outlined below, and label each disk clearly (e.g., Publisher Unit C Disk 1).

Unit and Location	Project File Supplied	Student Saves File As	Student Creates File
Disk 1			
Lessons	PB C-1.jpg		loftweb.htm

Unit and Location	Project File Supplied	Student Saves File As	Student Creates File
	PB C-2.doc		loftweb.pub
	PB C-3.pub		
Disk 2			
Skills Review	PB C-4.jpg		Folder: mediarec
	PB C-5.doc		recsite.pub
	PB C-6.pub		recsite.htm
			Folder: fund
			fund.htm
Disk 3			
Independent Challenge 1	PB C-7.doc		karaoke.pub
			Folder: karaoke
			karaoke.htm
Disk 4			
Independent Challenge 2	PB C-8.doc		Folder: jasmine
			jasmine.htm
Disk 5			
Independent Challenge 3			myweb.pub
			folder: mywebpg
			myweb.htm
Disk 6			
Independent Challenge 4			mycause.pub
			folder: my_cause
			mycause.htm
Disk 7			
Visual Workshop	PB C-9.doc		innsite.pub
			folder: inn
			innsite.htm

Glossary

Animated GIF File format used to display animations in Web pages.

Ask a Question box Text box at the top right side of the menu bar in which you can type a question to access the program's Help system.

AutoFit A formatting feature that automatically sizes text to fit in a frame.

Autoflow A feature that automatically flows text from one existing empty text frame to the next, asking for confirmation before it flows to the next frame.

Background Layer that appears behind every page in a publication where you put objects such as headers that you want repeated on each page.

Clip art Ready-made graphics available in the Clip Organizer that can be inserted in publications.

Clip Organizer Library of art, pictures, sounds, video clips, and animations shared by all Microsoft Office applications.

Color scheme A named set of five colors that can be applied consistently throughout a publication. There are 66 professionally selected color schemes provided in Publisher.

Connected text box A text box whose text flows either from or to another text box.

Continued notice A phrase that identifies where the overflow text continues from or continues to.

Design Gallery A collection of Publisher-designed objects such as logos, calendars, sidebars, Web page components, and other design elements that you can use to enhance your publications.

Design Set A group of sample designs provided by Publisher applied to a broad range of publication types including business cards, letterhead, and fax cover sheets to ensure a consistent and professional look.

Desktop publishing program A program for creating publications containing text and graphics.

Desktop workspace The area around the publication page you can use to store text and graphics prior to placing them in a publication.

Drop cap A specially formatted first letter of the first word of a paragraph.

Font The typeface or design of a set of characters (letters, numbers, symbols, and punctuation marks).

Font scheme A named set of two fonts, a major font and a minor font, that are applied consistently throughout a publication.

Font size The physical size of characters measured in units called points (pts).

Foreground The layer that sits on top of the background layer and consists of the objects that appear on a specific page of a publication.

Form control An item in a form that's used for gathering information from a user, such as a text box, list box, command button, or check box.

Frame An object that contains text or graphics and that can be moved or resized.

GIF The abbreviation for the graphic interchange format; the standard format for displaying images on Web pages.

Group To combine multiple objects into a single object so you can easily move and resize them as a unit.

Handles Small circles that appear around a selected object that you can drag to resize or rotate the selected object.

Header Text that prints at the top of each page in a publication.

Home page The first page that a visitor to a Web site usually sees. The home page usually links to other pages in the Web site, and other pages link back to it.

Host A location where you can store the files for a Web site.

Hyperlink An object or link (a filename, word, phrase, or graphic) in a document that, when clicked, opens another site or Web page.

Hypertext Markup Language (HTML) The common programming language used to create Web pages.

Internet A system of connected computers and computer networks located around the world by telephone lines, cables, satellites, and other telecommunications media.

Layout guides Nonprinting lines that appear in every page of your publication to help you to align text, pictures, and other objects into columns and rows so that your publication will have a consistent look across all pages.

Margin Perimeter of the page outside of which nothing will print.

Master page The page where you place any object that you want to repeat on every page of a publication.

Menu bar A bar beneath the title bar that lists the menus that contain the program's commands.

Navigation bar The bar that provides a set of links to pages in a Web site.

Nudge Feature that allows you to move an object one small increment at a time.

Object In Publisher, any element in a publication that contains text or graphics and that can be moved or resized.

Object Position indicator An indicator on the status bar used to precisely position an object.

Object Size indicator An indicator on the status bar used to accurately gauge the size of an object.

Office Assistant An animated character that appears to offer tips, answer questions, and provide access to the program's Help system.

Overflow text Text that won't fit in a text frame.

Pack and Go Wizard A wizard that lets you package your publication to take to another computer or to a commercial printing service.

Page Navigation buttons The buttons at the bottom of the publication window that are used to jump to a specific page in your publication.

Picture caption Text that appears next to, above, or below a picture to describe or elaborate on the picture.

Publication A file created in Publisher.

Publication Gallery A pane that displays thumbnails of Publisher ready-made designs for the selected category in the New Publication task pane.

Publication page A visual representation of your publication that appears in the publication window.

Publication window The area that includes the workspace for the publication page or pages and a desktop workspace for storing text and graphics prior to placing them in your publication.

Publishing a Web site Process of making a Web site available to World Wide Web users by storing all files on a web server.

Pull quote A quotation from a story that is pulled out and treated like a graphic.

Rotation handle A green circular handle at the top of a selected object that you can drag to rotate the selected object to any angle between 0 to 360 degrees.

Rulers Vertical and horizontal bars in the publication window marked in inches, centimeters, picas, or points that help you position text and graphics in your publications.

Ruler guides Nonprinting lines that appear on a single page of your publication that help you align text, pictures, and other objects into columns and rows.

Scroll bars Bars at the right and bottom edges of the publication window used to view different parts of your publication not currently visible in the window.

Selection handles Small boxes or circles that appear around a selected object that are used for moving and resizing the object.

Sidebar Text that is set apart from the major text but in some way relates to that text.

Status bar The bar at the bottom of the publication window that indicates the current page, the position and size of the selected object in a publication.

Story A single article that is contained in either one text box or a series of connected text boxes.

Table Information that appears in columns and rows for quick reference and analysis.

Task pane A window that provides quick access to the common tasks organized by categories such as Publication Designs, Web Site Options, Insert Clip Art, Color Schemes, and Font Schemes to help you perform tasks in Publisher.

Template A model for a publication that contains formatting specifications for text, fonts, and colors that can be used as a basis for a new publication.

Text box A type of frame that contains text, and that can be moved or resized.

Text flow icon An icon that appears in a text box to indicate whether the text in the text box flows to another text box, or whether it fits in the text box.

Text style A set of formatting characteristics that you can quickly apply to text on a paragraph-by-paragraph basis.

Title bar The bar at the top of the publication window that displays the names of the program and current publication.

Toggle key A key that switches between two options – press once to turn the option on, press again to turn it off.

Toolbar A bar that contains buttons you can click to perform commands.

Two-page spread Pages that will face each other when the publication is printed.

Web browser Software used to view Web pages and Web sites.

Web forms Forms that provide an easy way for a user to submit information via the Web.

Web page A document that is stored on the Web or an intranet and viewed on a computer using a Web browser.

Web publication A publication that you can convert to either a Web page or a Web site.

Web server A computer with a permanent connection to the Internet; it runs Web server software and it makes Web pages available to anyone with Web access.

Web site Group of associated Web pages that are linked together with hyperlinks.

Wizard An interactive series of dialog boxes that guides you through a task.

WordArt Text that is treated as a graphic.

World Wide Web (WWW) A collection of electronic documents available to people around the world via the Internet, commonly referred to as the Web.

Wrapping The flow of text around an object rather than over it or behind it.

Index

Index